DATE DUE			
SFPL AUG 21 '93			
SFPL SEP 11 '93			
SFPL OCT 02 '93			
DEC 21 1993			
JAN 11 1994			
APR 10 1994 SEP 3 1994			
MAY -2 1997			

891.6 J135s

402303

STUDIES IN EARLY
CELTIC NATURE POETRY

LONDON
Cambridge University Press
FETTER LANE

NEW YORK · TORONTO
BOMBAY · CALCUTTA · MADRAS
Macmillan

TOKYO
Maruzen Company Ltd

All rights reserved

STUDIES IN EARLY
CELTIC NATURE POETRY

BY

KENNETH JACKSON, M.A.

*Fellow of St John's College, Cambridge,
and Assistant Lecturer (in Celtic)
in the Faculty of Archaeology
and Anthropology*

CAMBRIDGE
AT THE UNIVERSITY PRESS
1935

891.6
J135R
402303

PRINTED IN GREAT BRITAIN

CONTENTS

Preface — page vii

Abbreviations — xi

PART I

THE IRISH POEMS — page 1
    Notes to the Irish Poems — 35

THE WELSH POEMS — 50
    Notes to the Welsh Poems — 76

PART II

Introduction — page 79

CHAPTERS

I. HERMIT POETRY — page 93

II. ELEGY AND FENIAN POETRY — 110

III. GNOMIC POETRY — 127

IV. SEASONAL POETRY — 149

V. PROBLEMS OF WELSH NATURE POETRY — 176
    Note. The Later Welsh Poets — 193

List of Chief Works Mentioned — 199

Index to Part II — 201

PREFACE

The Irish and Welsh poems described in this study constitute what has come to be called the "early Celtic nature poetry".[1] The name has been the accepted one for these poems as a whole because they deal to a greater or less extent with external nature, though much is obviously not what we should call real nature poetry at all; and this general description has tended to obscure the fact that the poems are actually very diverse in character. So much is this the case that writers have ascribed them all to the only group of poets who were at all obviously the authors of some. In the following pages an attempt is made to discover from internal evidence, and from such external evidence as is to be had, what really are the different kinds of poetry that have been included under this name, what sort of people composed them, and what was their purpose. The comparative method is freely used where other literatures in much the same stage of evolution, such as the Anglo-Saxon, can offer useful parallels. I have limited myself to the literatures of the early period in both Celtic languages, that is to say up to about the twelfth and thirteenth centuries, because after that time foreign influences were making themselves felt in Welsh, and in Irish the nature poetry was losing its earlier spontaneity. Actually the period includes most, certainly the best, of Irish nature poetry, and a good deal of the Welsh; but it excludes the incomparable nature poems of Dafydd ab Gwilym, which would need a separate study to themselves and have very little connection with the poetry dealt with here.

Both the Irish and the Welsh poems have been edited

[1] This use of "Celtic" is a convenient shortening for "Irish and Welsh"; properly the word belongs only to linguistics.

more or less satisfactorily in the original by now, and are easily accessible to scholars; references to these editions will be found in the Notes. It was necessary, however, to make new translations of all of them. Some of the Irish poems had not been put into English before, and progress in Celtic scholarship has made previous renderings of others out of date in some respects; while the Welsh poems had never been properly translated at all, for the versions given in W. F. Skene's *Four Ancient Books of Wales* are often badly astray. The translations given here are intended to be as literal as is consistent with grammatical English; it is hoped that the reader will find adequate justification in the notes to the Irish poems for the more important passages where they differ from those of previous writers. For the Welsh poems, he is referred on page 76 to the various published editions.

The following signs are used in translating: a word or phrase between two daggers indicate that the translation is tentative; a blank between two daggers, that no translation has been attempted; a row of dots, that something is missing in the manuscript; and a row of dots between verses, that one or more verses have been left out in the translation.

The work of which my book *Early Welsh Gnomic Poems* and the present volume are the outcome was undertaken in 1933–34 as research under the terms of the "Allen" scholarship, and I should like to take this opportunity of thanking the electors for making it possible for me to carry it out; also of expressing my gratitude to the Master and Fellows of St John's College for electing me to a Fellowship on its completion. My thanks are likewise due to the friends who have so kindly helped me in various ways. Above all to Professor Ifor Williams for his invaluable and very generous assistance with the difficult Welsh poems, and for his help in reading a proof; to Professor Osborn Bergin, to

PREFACE

whose unrivalled scholarship I am much indebted in this and other ways, for very kindly helping me with the chief cruxes in the Irish poems; to Dr Robin Flower for many illuminating hints and suggestions and much very welcome encouragement; to Mr Gerard Murphy for reading the book in manuscript and for his sympathetic criticism and support; and to Mr M. P. Charlesworth for reading a proof and offering some useful hints. I wish too to thank Professor and Mrs H. M. Chadwick, to whose inspiration this book owes a great deal, for suggesting the subject; the Principal of the University College of Wales for the friendly interest he has taken in the work; and the authorities of the Royal Irish Academy for allowing me the privilege of using their collection of Irish lexicographical slips. Also the Syndics of the University Press for undertaking the publication and their staff for the very efficient way in which it has been carried out.

KENNETH JACKSON

Cambridge
July 1935

ABBREVIATIONS[1]

(The Irish and Welsh poems are numbered in large Roman figures and capital letters respectively, and references to verse and line are given in Arabic figures and small Roman figures; e.g. III. 10, ii; E, 15, iii).

ACL = Archiv für Celtische Lexicographie.
Anc. I. = K. Meyer, Selections from Ancient Irish Poetry.
BBC = The Black Book of Carmarthen (references to J. G. Evans' edition by folio and line).
BBCh = The Black Book of Chirk.
BBCh prov. = The proverb list in the Black Book of Chirk (see p. 139).
BDict. = O. J. Bergin, Dictionary of the Irish Language.
Bruch. = K. Meyer, Bruchstücke der älteren Lyrik Irlands.
BT = The Book of Taliesin (references to J. G. Evans' edition by page and line).
Bull. = The Bulletin of the Board of Celtic Studies.
CB = A. J. Schmeller, Carmina Burana.
CLH = Ifor Williams, Canu Llywarch Hen.
Conts. = K. Meyer, Contributions to Irish Lexicography.
Cott. Gn. = The Anglo-Saxon gnomic poem in the Cotton Collection (see p. 128).
DDG = Ifor Williams, Detholion o Gywyddau Dafydd ab Gwilym.
Engl. Clyw. = The Englynion y Clyweit (see p. 139).
EWGP = Kenneth Jackson, Early Welsh Gnomic Poems.
Ex. Gn. = The Anglo-Saxon gnomic poem in the Exeter Book (see p. 128).
Four Songs = K. Meyer, Four Old Irish Songs of Summer and Winter.
Handbuch II = R. Thurneysen, Handbuch des Altirischen, vol. II.
Hendre G. = J. Morris-Jones and T. H. Parry-Williams, Llawysgrif Hendregadredd.
Ir. T. = E. Windisch and W. Stokes, Irische Texte.

[1] For full titles see List of Chief Works Mentioned.

ABBREVIATIONS

IW = Ifor Williams.
JGE = J. Gwenogvryn Evans.
JMJ = Sir John Morris-Jones.
KM = Kuno Meyer.
LL = The Book of Leinster.
Luibh. = F. E. Hogan, Luibhleabhrán.
MA = The Myvyrian Archaeology of Wales, second edition.
MD = T. F. O'Rahilly, Measgra Dánta.
Onom. = F. E. Hogan, Onomasticon Goedelicum.
Origines = A. Jeanroy, Les Origines de la Poésie Lyrique en France.
Pen. 17 prov. = The proverb list in Peniarth MS. 17 (see p. 139).
RBH = The Red Book of Hergest (references to J. G. Evans' edition of the Poetry, by column and line).
RC = Revue Celtique.
Recherches = Th. Chotzen, Recherches sur la Poésie de Dafydd ab Gwilym.
RIA = The Royal Irish Academy.
S = The Irish lexicographical slips in the Royal Irish Academy.
Thes. Pal. = W. Stokes and J. Strachan, Thesaurus Palaeohibernicus.
WB prov. = The proverb list in the White Book of Rhydderch (see p. 139).
Welsh Bard = Glyn Davies, The Welsh Bard and the Poetry of External Nature.
ZCP = Zeitschrift für Celtische Philologie.

Part One

THE POEMS

THE IRISH POEMS

I. *The Ivy Bower*

1. My little hut in Tuaim Inbhir,
   a mansion would not be more ingenious,
   with its stars to my wish,
   with its sun, with its moon.

2. It was Gobban that made it
   —that the tale may be told you—
   my darling, God of heaven,
   was the thatcher that roofed it.

3. A house in which rain does not fall,
   a place in which spears are not feared,
   as open as if in a garden
   and it without a wall about it.

II

1. The woodland thicket overtops me,
   the blackbird sings me a lay, praise I will not conceal:
   above my lined little booklet
   the trilling of birds sings to me.

2. The clear cuckoo sings to me, lovely discourse,
   in its grey cloak from the crest of the bushes;
   truly—may the Lord protect me!—
   well do I write under the forest wood.

III. *The Song of Manchín of Liath*

1. I wish, O Son of the living God,
   eternal ancient King,
   for a secret hut in the wilderness
   that it may be my dwelling.

2. A very blue shallow well
   to be beside it,
   a clear pool for washing away sins
   through the grace of the Holy Ghost.

3. A beautiful wood close by
   around it on every side
   for the nurture of many-voiced birds
   to shelter and hide it.

4. Facing the south for warmth,
   a little stream across its ground,
   a choice plot with abundant bounties
   which would be good for every plant.

5. A few sage disciples,
   I will tell their number,
   humble and obedient
   to pray to the King.

6. Four threes, three fours
   ready for every need,
   two sixes in the church
   both south and north.

7. Six couples as well
   besides me myself
   praying through the long ages
   to the King who moves the sun.

8. A lovely church decked with linen,
   a dwelling for God of heaven;
   then, bright candles
   over the holy white scriptures.

9. One room to go to
   for the tendance of the body,
   without ribaldry, without boasting,
   without meditation of evil.

10. This is the housekeeping I would get,
    I would choose it without concealing,
    fragrant fresh leeks, hens,
    salmon, trout, bees.

11. My fill of clothing and food
    from the King of good fame,
    and for me to be sitting for a time
    praying to God in every place.

IV

1. The skilled lark calls,
   I go outside to watch it
   that I may see its gaping beak
   above against the dappled cloudy sky.

2. I will sing my psalms
   for holy bright heaven
   that I may be shielded from harm,
   for the purging of my sins.

V

*   *   *   *   *

1. I have a hut in the wood,
   none knows it but my Lord;
   an ash tree this side, a hazel beyond,
   a great tree on a mound enfolds it.

2. Two heathery door-posts for support
   and a porch of honeysuckle;
   around its close the wood sheds
   its mast upon fat swine.

3. The size of my hut, small yet not small,
   a place of familiar paths;
   the she-bird in dress of blackbird colour
   sings a melodious strain from its gable.

4. The stags of Druim Rolach leap
   out of its stream of trim meadows;
   from them red Roigne can be seen,
   noble Mucraimhe and Maonmagh.

5. A little hidden lowly hut
   which owns the paths †that you may reach†;
   you will not go with me to see it,
   I shall tell of its †   †

6. The concealing tresses of a green-trunked yew
   which upholds †the sky†;
   fair is the place; the green wall of an oak
   against the storm.

7. A tree of apples of great bounty
   like a mansion, stout;
   a pretty bush, thick as a fist, of small hazel-nuts,
   branching and green.

8. An excellent spring, a cup of noble water
   to drink;
   water-cresses sprout, yew-berries,
   ivy bushes as big as a man.

9. Around it lie tame swine,
   goats, boars,
   wild swine, grazing deer,
   a badger's brood.

10. A peaceful company, a grave host of the countryside,
an assembly to my house;
foxes come to meet them,
delightful it is.

11. Excellent princes come to my house,
a nimble gathering;
pure water, evergreen bushes,
salmon, trout.

12. A bough of rowan, black sloes
of the dark blackthorn,
plenty of food, acorns, spare berries,
† †, milk.

13. A clutch of eggs, honey, produce of wild onions,
God has sent it,
sweet apples, red whortleberries,
crowberries.

14. Beer with herbs, a dish of strawberries,
coloured dainties,
haws, yewberries,
sloes, nuts.

15. A cup † †, goodly hazel-nuts,
early young corn,
brown oak-bushes, manes of briar,
fine †sweet-tangle†.

16. In pleasant summer with its coloured mantle,
good-tasting savour,
pignuts, wild marjoram, fresh leeks,
green purity.

17. The songs of the bright redbreasted folk,
a beloved movement,
the carol of the thrush, familiar cuckoos
above my house.

18. Swarms of bees, chafers, soft music of the world,
    a gentle humming;
    wild geese, ducks, shortly before the beginning of
        winter;
    music of the dark torrent.
19. A nimble songster, the combative brown wren
    from the hazel bough,
    speckled hooded birds, woodpeckers
    in a great multitude.
20. Fair white birds come, cranes, seagulls,
    the sea sings to them,
    no mournful music; brown fowl
    out of the red heather.
21. Lowing of heifers in summer,
    brightest of weather,
    not bitter or toilsome over the mellow plain,
    delightful, mild.
22. The voice of the wind against its branchy wood
    grey with cloud;
    cascades of the river, the swan's song,
    lovely music.
23. A beautiful pine makes music to me
    that is not hired;
    though I sing to Christ I fare no worse
    than you do.
24. Though you delight in your own pleasures
    greater than all wealth,
    for my part I am thankful for what is given me
    from my dear Christ.
25. Without an hour of quarrel, without the noise of strife
    which disturbs you,
    grateful to the Prince who gives every good
    to me in my hut.

VI

1. Delightful I think it to be in the bosom of an isle
   on the crest of a rock,
   that I may look there on the manifold
   face of the sea.

2. That I may see its heavy waves
   over the glittering ocean
   as they chant a melody to their Father
   on their eternal course.

3. That I may see its smooth strand of clear headlands,
   no gloomy thing;
   that I may hear the voice of the wondrous birds,
   a joyful course.

4. That I may hear the sound of the shallow waves
   against the rocks;
   that I may hear the cry beside the churchyard,
   the roar of the sea.

5. That I may see its splendid flocks of birds
   over the full-watered ocean;
   that I may see its mighty whales,
   greatest of wonders.

6. That I may see its ebb and its flood-tide
   in its flow;
   that this should be my name, a secret I declare,
   "He who turned his back on Ireland."

7. That contrition of heart should come upon me
   when I look on it;
   that I may bewail my many sins
   difficult to declare.

8. That I may bless the Lord
who has power over all,
heaven with its crystal orders of angels,
earth, ebb, flood tide.

9. That I may pore on one of my books,
good for my soul,
a while kneeling for beloved heaven,
a while at psalms.

10. A while meditating upon the Prince of Heaven,
holy is the redemption,
a while at labour not too heavy;
it would be delightful!

11. A while gathering dilisk from the rock,
a while fishing,
a while giving food to the poor,
a while in my cell.

12. The counsel which is best before God
may He confirm it to me,
may the King, whose servant I am, not desert me,
may He not deceive me.

VII

There is here above the brotherhood
a bright tall glossy yew;
the melodious bell sends out a clear keen note
in St Columba's church.

VIII

The little bird has given a whistle
from the point of its bright yellow beak;
the blackbird from the yellow-tipped bough
sends forth its note over Loch Laoigh.

IX

The bird that calls from the willow,
lovely is its little beak with its clear call,
the melodious yellow bill of the jet-black hardy bird;
a lively tune is sung, the blackbird's note.

X

Ah, blackbird, it is well for thee
where thy nest is in the brake;
hermit that dost not clang a bell,
melodious, soft, and peaceful is thy call.

XI

1. Young stag, little belling one,
   melodious little bleater,
   sweet to me is the lowing
   that you make in the glen.

2. Home-sickness for my little dwelling
   has fallen upon my mind,
   the herds in the lowlands,
   the deer on the mountain.

3. Oak, bushy, leafy,
   you are high above trees;
   hazel-bush, little branchy one
   sweet-smelling with hazel-nuts.

4. Alder, you are not spiteful,
   lovely is your colour,
   you are not like the prickly hawthorn
   where you are in the gully.

5. Blackthorn, little thorny one,
   black little sloe-bush;
   water-cress, little green-topped one
   on the brink of the blackbird's well.

6. Saxifrage of the pathway,
   you are sweetest of herbs;
   cress, very green one;
   plant where the strawberry grows.

7. Apple-tree, little apple-tree,
   violently everyone shakes you;
   rowan, little berried one,
   lovely is your bloom.

8. Bramble, little humped one,
   you do not grant fair terms,
   you do not desist from tearing me
   till you are sated with blood.

9. Yew, little yew,
   you are conspicuous in graveyards;
   ivy, little ivy,
   you are familiar in the dark wood.

10. Holly, little shelterer,
    shutter against the wind;
    ash, baneful,
    weapon in the hand of a warrior.

11. Birch, smooth, blessed,
    proud, melodious,
    lovely is each entangled branch
    at the top of your crest.

12. Aspen a-trembling,
    at times when I hear
    its leaves rustling
    I think it is the foray.

*   *   *   *   *

13. If I were to search alone
    the mountains of the dark earth
    I would rather have the room for a single hut
    in proud Glen Bolcán.

14. Good is its clear blue water,
    good its clean stern wind,
    good its cress-green watercress,
    best its deep brooklime.

15. Good its lasting ivy,
    good its bright merry willow,
    good its yewy yew,
    best its melodious birch.

* * * * *

XII

1. Gloomy is this life,
   to be without a soft bed,
   a cold frosty dwelling,
   harshness of snowy wind.

2. Cold icy wind,
   faint shadow of a feeble sun,
   the shelter of a single tree
   on the top of the level moor.

3. Enduring the shower,
   stepping along deer-paths,
   traversing greenswards
   on a morning of raw frost.

* * * *

XIII

* * * * *

1. This is my nightly sustenance,
   ever the gleanings of my hands,
   what I pluck in dark oak-groves
   of herbs and abundant fruits.

2. Splendid blaeberries are my delight,
   they are sweeter than soft shoots;
   brooklime, seaweed, they are delightful to me,
   the herbage and the watercress.

3. Apples, berries, nuts of the goodly hazel,
   blackberries, acorns from the oaktree,
   raspberries, the due of generosity,
   haws of the prickly sharp hawthorn.

4. Wood-sorrel, sorrel, fine wild garlic,
   and clean-topped watercress,
   together they drive starvation from me,
   berries of the moor, root of the wild onion.

* * * * *

XIV

The fort whereon I am
in which there is a little spring with a bright cup,
melodious was the sound of the wood of blackbirds
about the fort of Fiacha mac Monche.

XV

1. Well of Tráigh Dhá Bhan,
   lovely is your pure-topped cress;
   since your verdure has become neglected
   no growth has been allowed to your brooklime.

2. Your trout out by your banks,
   your wild swine in your wilderness,
   the deer of your crags fine for hunting,
   your dappled red-breasted fawns.

3. Your mast on the tips of your trees,
   your fish in the mouths of your streams,
   lovely is the colour of your sprigs of arum lily,
   green brook in the wooded hollow!

* * * * *

XVI

1. Arran of the many stags,
   the sea reaches to its shoulder;
   island where companies are fed,
   ridges whereon blue spears are reddened.

2. Wanton deer upon its peaks,
   mellow blaeberries on its heaths,
   cold water in its streams,
   mast upon its brown oaks.

3. Hunting dogs there, and hounds,
   blackberries and sloes of the dark blackthorn,
   dense thorn-bushes in its woods,
   stags astray among its oak-groves.

4. Gathering of purple lichen on its rocks,
grass without blemish on its slopes;
over its fair shapely crags
Gambolling of dappled fawns leaping.

5. Smooth is its lowland, fat its swine,
pleasant its fields, a tale to be believed;
its nuts on the boughs of its hazel-wood,
sailing of long galleys past it.

6. It is delightful when fine weather comes,
trout under the banks of its streams,
seagulls answer each other round its white cliff;
delightful at all times is Arran.

XVII

1. High and delightful hill
to which the fair Fiana used to come,
there was wont to be a very great encampment
upon you, and a band of fine young men.

2. This was our portion for to tell
when we used to come to the high smooth level,
lovely blackberries, haws,
nuts from the hazels of Cantyre.

3. Shoots of the prickly bramble,
stalks of faultless garlic;
every May Day we would eat
smooth shoots and tops of cress.

4. Birds from the depths of the oakwoods
used to reach the cooking-pit of the Fiana,
dappled martens from Berramain,
little nests from the peaks of the mountains.

5. Swift salmon of Lindmuine,
   eels of the noble Shannon,
   woodcocks of Fidrenn,
   otters from the recesses of the Deel.

6. Fish of the watery sea
   from the coasts of Dursey and Beare,
   meadhbhán of bright Whiddy
   dilisk from the havens of Clear.

7. Mac Lugach was wont
   to swim the Loingse with its lakes;
   we used to come in host and multitude
   to your side yonder, hill.

8. I and far-renowned Oisín
   used to journey in the prows of coracles;
   I got peril of the green sea
   about the waves and the hills.

XVIII

1. Cold is the winter, wind has risen,
   the vehement wanton stag arises;
   not warm to-night is the whole mountain
   though the ardent stag is belling.

2. The stag of Sliabh Cairn of the assemblies
   does not lay his side to the ground,
   the stag of the crest of cold Echtge
   listens not less to the music of the wolf pack.

3. I, Caoilte, and brown Diarmaid,
   and nimble Oscar,
   used to hear the music of the wolf pack
   at the end of the very cold night.

4. It is well sleeps the brown stag
   with his body close to the sharp rock,
   as if he were under Tonn Tuaighe
   at the end of the very cold night.

5. To-day I am an aged old man,
   I know but a few folk,
   yet I used to brandish a pointed spear fiercely
   on a cold icy morning.

6. I give thanks to the King of Heaven,
   to the Son of Mary the Virgin,
   I used to bring great silence on a host
   though to-night I fare very coldly.

XIX

1. You shall have in Brocc Ross,
   O Finn of the battle,
   whortleberries of the bog,
   fat of the swine of Slánga.

2. Acorns from the wilderness,
   a steak of the porpoise,
   birds of Airer Lemna,
   salmon from the bosom of the Barrow.

3. Roast meat of Cantyre,
   fish of the mouth of the Feale,
   venison of Cnoc Cláire,
   fat of the badger of Beare.

4. Nuts from Lettir Faelchon,
   from Fid Daruba,
   sunny blackberries
   of Sliabh Dá Duma.

5. The lovely apples
from the woods of Cua,
the sloes from Éibhle,
the wood of Fua of level glens.

6. Strawberries from Slíabh Bairche
you shall have in pleasant wise,
little fawns on spits
from the woods of Cáibde.

* * * *

XX

Slíabh Cua, haunt of wolves, rugged and dark,
the wind wails about its glens,
wolves howl around its chasms;
the fierce brown deer bells
in Autumn around it,
the crane screams over its crags.

XXI

1. Benn Boilbin that is sad to-day,
peak that was shapely and best of form,
at that time, son of Calpurnius,
it was lovely to be upon its crest.

2. Many were the dogs and the ghillies,
the cry of the bugle and the hound,
and the mighty heroes that were upon your rampart,
O high peak of the contests.

3. It was haunted by cranes in the night,
and heath-fowl on its moors,
with the tuning of small birds
it was delightful to be listening to them.

4. The cry of the hounds in its glens,
   the wonderful echo,
   and each of the Fiana
   with lovely dogs on the leash.

5. Many in the wood were the gleaners
   from the fair women of the Fiana,
   its berries of sweet taste,
   raspberries and blackberries.

6. Mellow purple blaeberries,
   tender cress and cuckoo-flower;
   and the curly-haired fair-headed maids,
   sweet was the sound of their singing.

7. It was cause to be joyous
   to be looking and listening
   to the lonesome scream of the eagle,
   to the murmur of the otters
   and the talk of the foxes.

8. The blackbird at Inbher Sceiche
   singing most sweetly,
   I swear to you, Patrick,
   that was a delightful place.

9. We were on this hill
   seven companies of the Fiana;
   to-night my friends are few,
   and is not my tale pitiful to you?

XXII

1. The delight of handsome MacCumhaill
   was to listen to the shout on Druim Dearg,
   to sleep by the stream of Assaroe,
   and to hunt the deer of Galway of the havens.

2. The trilling of the blackbird of Leitir Laoigh,
   the Wave of Rudhraighe striking on the strand,
   the belling of the stag of Maonmagh,
   the bleat of the fawn of Gleann Dá Mháil.

3. The cry of the hunt of Sliabh Crot,
   the sound of the stags about Sliabh Cua,
   the cries of seagulls in Erris yonder,
   the scream of ravens above the hosts.

4. The tossing of the hulls of ships upon the wave,
   the howl of the wolf-packs of Drum Lis,
   the barkings of Bran on Cnoc an Aír,
   and the laughter of the streams about Slemish.

5. The call of Oscar going to hunt,
   the voice of hounds on the hillside of the Fiana,
   to be sitting among the poets,
   that was his wonted delight.

XXIII

1. Sweet it is, blackbird of Doire an Chairn,
   I have not heard in the world at all
   tune that was sweeter than your tune,
   and you sitting on your nest.

   *   *   *   *   *   *

2. Doire an Chairn, the wood yonder in the west,
   where the Fiana used to take repose;
   on its fair and graceful trees
   there the blackbird used to be.

3. The warbling of the blackbird of Doire an Chairn,
   the belling of the stag of Aill na gCaor,
   music at which Fionn would fall soon asleep;
   ducks of Loch na dTrí gCaol.

4. Heath-fowl about Cruachan of Connaught,
   the cry of the otter of Druim Dá Loch,
   the screams of the eagle of Gleann na bhFuath,
   singing of the cuckoos of Cnoc na Scoth.

5. Cries of the hound of Gleann Caoin,
   and the shriek of the blind eagle of the hunts,
   roar of the wave coming early
   in upon Tráigh na gCloch nDearg.

6. While Fionn was living and the Fiana
   dearer to them was the mountain than the church;
   sweet they thought the note of blackbirds,
   tinklings of bells they did not think sweet.

XXIV

1. Delightful to be on the Hill of Howth,
   very sweet to be above its white sea,
   the perfect fertile hill, home of ships,
   the vine-grown pleasant brave peak.

2. The peak where Fionn and the Fiana used to be,
   the peak where used to be horns and drinking-cups,
   the peak where O'Duinn sang songs
   to Gráinne in stress of exile.

3. The peak bright-knolled beyond all hills,
   with its hilltop round and green and rugged,
   the hill full of swordsmen, and wild garlic and trees,
   the peak many-coloured, full of beasts, wooded.

4. The peak that is loveliest throughout the soil of Ireland,
the bright peak above the sea of gulls,
it is a hard step for me to leave it,
lovely Hill of pleasant Howth.

XXV

1. May Day, fair season,
perfect is colour then;
blackbirds sing a full lay
if there be a slender beam of day.

2. The loud hardy cuckoo calls,
welcome noble summer!
The bitterness of bad weather subsides,
the branching wood is a †   † hedge.

3. Summer brings low the little stream,
the swift herd makes for the water,
the long hair of the heather spreads out,
the weak white cotton-grass flourishes.

4. †   †,
the smooth sea flows,
season when the ocean falls asleep;
blossom covers the world.

5. Bees, whose strength is small, carry
a goodly load reaped from flowers,
cattle carry mud up the mountain,
the ant makes a rich meal.

6. The harp of the wood plays melody,
the sail gathers—perfect peace;
colour has settled on every hill;
haze on the lake of full waters.

7. The corncrake clacks, a strenuous bard,
   the high pure waterfall sings
   a greeting to the warm pool;
   rustling of rushes has come.

8. Light swallows dart on high,
   loud music encircles the knoll,
   the tender rich mast flourishes,
   the stuttering mire discourses.

9. The †black† bog is like the raven's coat,
   the loud cuckoo makes greeting,
   the speckled fish leaps,
   strong is the †   † of the swift warrior.

10. Man thrives, the maiden flourishes
    in her fine strong prime;
    fair is every wood from crest to ground,
    fair each great goodly plain.

11. Delightful is the season's splendour,
    rough winter has gone,
    bright is every fruitful wood,
    a joyous peace is summer.

12. A flock of birds settles
    †in the midst   †
    the green field †   †
    in which is a brisk bright stream.

13. A mad ardour upon you to race horses,
    the serried host is ranged around,
    a bright shaft has been loosed into the land
    so that the iris is gold beneath it.

14. A timid persistent frail creature
    sings at the top of his voice,
    the lark chants clear tidings;
    excellent May Day of quiet colours!

XXVI

1. Summer has come, healthy and free,
   at which the dark wood becomes bowed;
   the slender nimble deer leaps
   when the path of seals is smooth.

2. The cuckoo sings sweet soft music
   at which there is tranquil unbroken sleep,
   gentle birds hop about the knoll
   and swift grey stags.

3. Heat has laid hold on the repose of the deer,
   pleasant is the cry of active packs;
   the white stretch of the strand smiles
   where the brisk sea is turbulent.

4. The noise of wanton winds in the top
   of the dark oakwood of Drum Daill;
   the noble hornless herd-runs
   to which Cuan Wood is a shelter.

5. Green bursts out on every plant,
   wooded is the copse of the green oak-grove;
   summer has come, winter has gone,
   tangled hollies wound the hound.

6. The hardy blackbird sings a strain,
   to whom the thorny wood is a heritage;
   the sad turbulent sea is sleeping,
   the speckled salmon leaps.

7. The sun smiles over every land,
   I am freed from the brood of †   †;
   hounds bark, stags assemble,
   ravens flourish, summer has come.

XXVII

1. I have tidings for you;
   the stag bells,
   winter snows,
   summer has gone.

2. Wind high and cold,
   the sun low,
   short its course,
   the sea running high.

3. Crimson the bracken,
   it has lost its shape,
   the wild goose has raised
   its accustomed cry.

4. Cold has seized
   the birds' wings,
   season of ice,
   these are my tidings.

XXVIII

Winter has come with scantiness,
lakes have flooded the land,
frosts crumble the leaves,
the merry wave mutters.

XXIX

1. Deathly cold!
   The storm is greater than ever;
   each gleaming furrow is a river,
   and every ford is a full lake.

2. Big as a great sea is each turbulent lake,
a multitude is each keen scanty band,
the rain-drop is as big as a shield boss,
each flake is as big as a white wether-skin.

3. Each †dark† puddle is as big as a pit,
each level is a cairn, each bog a wood;
the bird-flocks do not get shelter,
white snow reaches right up to the fork.

4. Sudden frost has closed the roads
after keen battle round Colt's pillar;
the storm has spread on every side,
so that none say anything but "Cold!"

XXX

1. Cold, cold,
cold to-night is wide Magh Luirg;
the snow is higher than a mountain,
the deer cannot get at its food.

2. Deathly cold;
the storm has spread on every side;
each sloping furrow is a river
and every ford is a full mere.

3. Each full lake is a great sea,
and each mere is a full lake;
horses cannot get across the ford of Ross,
no more can two feet get there.

4. The fishes of Ireland are a-roving,
there is not a strand whereon the wave does not dash,
there is not a town in the land,
no bell is to be heard, no crane calls.

5. The wolves of Cuan Wood do not get
repose or sleep in the lair of wolves;
the little wren does not find
shelter for her nest on the slope of Lon.

6. The keen wind and the cold ice
have broken out on the company of little birds;
the blackbird does not find a bank she would like,
shelter for her side in the woods of Cuan.

7. Snug is our cauldron on its hook,
ramshackle the hut on the slope of Lon;
snow has crushed the wood here,
it is difficult to climb up Benn Bó.

8. The eagle of brown Glen Ridhe
gets affliction from the bitter wind;
great is her misery and her suffering,
the ice will get into her beak.

9. It is foolish for you—take heed of it—
to rise from quilt and feather-bed;
there is much ice on every ford;
that is why I say "Cold".

XXXI A

A good tranquil season is Autumn;
there is occupation then for everyone
throughout the very short days.
Dappled fawns from the side of the hinds,
the red stalks of the bracken shelter them;
stags run from knolls
at the belling of the deer-herd.

Sweet acorns in the high woods,
corn-stalks about cornfields
over the expanse of the brown earth.
Prickly thorn-bushes of the bramble
by the midst of the ruined court;
the hard ground is covered with heavy fruit.
Hazelnuts of good crop fall
from the huge old trees of mounds.

XXXI B

In the black season of deep winter
a storm of waves is roused
along the expanse of the world.
Sad are the birds of every meadow-plain
(except the ravens that feed on crimson blood)
at the clamour of fierce winter;
it is rough, black, dark, misty.
Dogs are vicious in cracking bones;
the iron pot is put on the fire
after the dark black day.

XXXI C

Raw and chilly is icy spring,
cold will arise in the wind;
the ducks of the watery pool are crying,
eager and †   † is the harsh-shrieking crane.
Wolves hear in the wilderness
the early rise of morning time;
birds awaken from †islands†,
many are the wild creatures from which they flee
out of the wood, out of the green grass.

XXXI D

A good season is †peaceful† summer;
luxuriant is the tall fine wood
which the whistle of the wind will not stir,
green is the plumage of the sheltering grove;
eddies swirl in the stream;
good is the warmth in the turf.

XXXII

1. A great tempest on the plain of Ler,[1]
   †   † bold across its high borders;
   wind has arisen, wild winter has slain us,
   it comes across the sea †   †
   the spear of the wild winter season has come upon it.

2. The deeds of the plain, the full plain of Ler,
   have brought alarm upon our wide host;
   except something more momentous than all, no less,
   what is there indeed more wonderful
   than the incomparable tremendous story?

3. When the wind sets from the east
   the mettle of the wave is roused;
   it desires to go over us westwards
   to the land where the sun sets,
   to the wild broad green sea.

4. When the wind sets from the north
   it desires that against the †   † sky
   against the southern world
   the dark stern wave should strive,
   should listen to the †   † song.

[1] I.e. the sea.

5. When the wind sets from the west
across the salt sea of rapid currents
it desires to go over us eastwards
to the sun-tree † †,
into the wide far-reaching sea.

6. When the wind sets from the south
across the land of the Saxons of stout shields
the wave strikes the island of Scit,
it has reached up to the peak of Caladnet,
and pounds the grey-green Shannon.

7. The ocean is full, the sea is in flood,
lovely is the home of ships;
the sandy wind has made eddies
around Inbher na dá Ainmech,
swift is the rudder upon the wide sea.

8. Not snug it is, a wild troubled sleep,
with feverish triumph, with furious strife;
the swan's hue †is upon the home†
of the Irish and their people,
the hair of the wife of Manannán[1] is tossed about.

9. The wave with mighty force
has come across each wide dark river-mouth,
wind has come, white winter has slain us,
about Cantyre, about the land of Scotland,
a flooded stream gushes out, mountainous and raging.

10. Son of God the Father, of vast hosts,
protect me from the horror of wild tempests!
Just Lord of the Feast,
only protect me from the mighty blast,
from Hell of tremendous tempests!

[1] I.e. the sea.

XXXIII

Bitter is the wind to-night,
it tosses the ocean's white tresses;
I do not fear the wild warriors of Norway
sailing on the Irish sea.

XXXIV. *On the Drowning of Conaing mac Aedain*

1. The great clear waves of the sea
   and the sand have covered them—
   into his frail little wicker coracle
   they flung themselves over Conaing.

2. The woman[1] has cast her white tresses
   into his coracle upon Conaing;
   hatefully she has smiled her smile
   to-day upon the Tree of Torta.

XXXV

Look before you to the north east
at the mighty sea, the home of creatures,
the dwelling of seals; wanton and splendid
it has taken on flood-tide.

XXXVI

It has broken us, it has crushed us, it has drowned us,
O King of the star-bright kingdom,
the wind has consumed us
as timber is consumed by crimson fire from heaven.

---

[1] I.e. the sea.

XXXVII

Cold is the night in Móin Mhór,
rain pours down that is not trifling,
a roaring with which the fresh wind laughs
howls over the sheltering wood.

XXXVIII

Ceann Easgrach of the orchards,
a dwelling for the meadow bees,
there is a glossy thicket upon its ground
where there is a drinking-cup of laths.

XXXIX

A conspicuous oakwood is Dairbre,
many strong young deer,
a rugged virile yew-tree,
straight, leafy, bushy.

XL

Gentle chorus, pleasant chorus, soft music of the world,
the cuckoo in the tree-tops, melodious is its voice;
motes appear in the sunbeams,
young creatures rejoice in the... of the moor.

XLI

1. Glen of fruits and fish and lakes,
   peaked hill of lovely wheat,
   it is distressful for me to think on it,
   glen full of bees, of the longhorned wild oxen.

2. Glen of cuckoos and thrushes and blackbirds,
   precious is its cover to every fox;
   glen full of wild garlic and watercress and woods,
   of shamrock and flowers, leafy and twisting-crested.

3. Sweet are the bellings of the brown-backed dappled deer
   under the oakwood over the bare hill top,
   gentle hinds that are timid
   lying hidden in the great-treed glen.

4. Glen of the rowan trees with scarlet berries
   with fruit praised by every flock of birds,
   a slumbrous paradise for the badgers
   in their quiet burrows with their young.

5. Glen of the blue-eyed hardy hawks,
   glen abounding in every fruit,
   glen of the ridged and jagged peaks,
   glen of blackberries and sloes and apples.

6. Glen of the sleek brown round-faced otters
   that are pleasant and active in fishing,
   many are the white-winged stately swans,
   and salmon breeding along the rocky brink.

7. Glen of the tangled branching yews,
   dewy glen with level lawn of kine,
   chalk-white starry sunny glen,
   glen of graceful pearl-like virtuous women.

NOTES

References are given as follows: (1) to the page or pages in this book where the poem is discussed, (2) the supposed date of the poem, (3) existing editions and translations, if any.

B = Professor Bergin's emendations or renderings of some of the difficult passages which he kindly discussed with me.

GM, in datings, = Gerard Murphy's dates to poems in his article "The Origin of Irish Nature Poetry" in *Studies*, March, 1931.

I

The Hermit describes his little hermitage. See pp. 97 and 122. Ninth century? Ed. Ir. T. I, pp. 318 ff.; ed. and tr. Thes. Pal. II, 294; ed. Thurneysen, Handbuch, II, pp. 39 ff. No context; but above the poem to the left is written in the MS. *Suibne Geilt*, to whom it is thus apparently attributed (see p. 122). The title, "The Ivy Bower" (*Barr edin*), is a scholiasm in the MS., and must refer to the ivy which grew over the cell in question.

II

A scribe writing in the wood. See pp. 80 and 100. Eighth or ninth century. Ed. and tr. Thes. Pal. II, p. 290; ed. Thurneysen, Handbuch, II, p. 39. No context.

1. i. thicket, lit. "fence".

III

Manchín (d. A.D. 665) describes his ideal of a hermit existence. See pp. 96, 98, 99, 103, and particularly 105. Ninth century (KM). Ed. and tr. KM, *Eriu*, I, pp. 38 ff. The poem is headed *Comad Manchín Leith*, i.e. the song of Manchín of Lemanaghan (see KM, *loc. cit.*).

2. i. well; MS. *huisín*, "a little lark"; B suggests read *huiscín* and tr. "a very blue shallow pond". Cf. *Eriu*, I, p. 138, l. 16, where Strachan expands MS. *uisī* as *uisci*, though *uisin* might be expected.

5. i. A few sage disciples (*uathad oclaich innide*), KM "a few men of sense"; but on *óclaoch*, cf. S, "disciple, follower (of a saint or religious leader); *as iatt cét-óclaigh battar acc Maodhócc*, Beth. Naem. n-Er. 264, § 226". *Innide*, from *inne* "sense"?

7. iv. the King who moves the sun (MS *in Rig ruithness grein*), KM "who makes the sun shine", taking *ruithness* as: *ruithnigim* "to shine". But there is no verb *ruithnim* "to make to shine" (S); read therefore *ruithes grein* from *roithim, ruithim*, causative of *reth-* (see H. Pedersen, *Vergleichende Grammatik der Keltischen Sprachen*, II, p. 600), and cf. *cen adrad rig roithes gréin*, LL 32 a, 29 and RC, XXIII, 316; and cf. Dante, *Paradiso*, Canto XXXIII, 145, *l' amor che move il sole e l' altre stelle*.

8. iii. candles, reading *sutralla* with KM in *Selections from Early Irish Poetry*, p. 11 (Dublin University Press, not published).

9. iii. without ribaldry, see KM, *Eriu*, I, *loc. cit.* without boasting (*cen indladuth*), so KM; cf. "*indládaim* = to boast (?); *a mendocán imráidim ocus dna cáin innláidim*" (S).

IV

See p. 100. Ed. and tr. Stokes, *Transactions of the Royal Irish Academy*, I, part 1, p. lxvi. No context. The two verses are in different metres.

V

King Guaire mac Colmáin Aidne, king of Connaught in the seventh century, comes to his brother Marbhán's hut and asks him in verse why he has left the world of men; Marbhán replies in verse 8 with the poem given here, and Guaire at the end admits how much he envies him (cf. p. 121).

See pp. 96, 98, 99, 100 and 107. Tenth century (KM). Ed. and tr. KM, *King and Hermit* (Nutt, 1901); tr. Anc. I. p. 47. The poem is full of difficulties and there is only one MS.; KM's translation sometimes tends to force the text to extract a meaning.

1. iv. a great tree on a mound (*bili ratha*), cf. poem XXXI A, 15, "the huge old trees of mounds" (*robilib rath*); the idea is that trees grow on ruined earthworks to a great age and size.

NOTES TO THE IRISH POEMS

3. ii. **a place of familiar paths**, reading *baili* with B; KM reads *ba ili* and tr. "many are its familiar paths", but *sett sognath* must be gen. pl.

4. ii. **out of its**, following MS. *assa*; KM's *issa* seems an unnecessary change.

   iii. **Roigne**, a plain in Kilkenny.

   iv. **Maonmagh**, a plain in co. Galway.

5. ii. **the paths that you may reach**, B, reading *set ro-is*, with *ro-ís*, 2nd sg. perfective pres. subj. act. of *icc-*.

   iii. **you will not go with me to see it** (*die dexin ni raga liom*), KM "to behold it will not be granted me", but *di* must be a preposition governing *dexin* here, "to its seeing".

   iv. *cetmouis?*

6. ii. **which upholds † the sky†**. So KM, but *cél* and *sín* cannot rhyme, and one of them must be wrong. On *cél* "sky", cf. Conts., s.v. *cél*.

   iii. **the green wall**, reading *maur glas* (B); KM *maurglas*, "the large green", would be a peculiar construction.

8. i–ii. **a cup of noble water** (*es ouisci uais*), KM "and princely water", but cf. B.Dict., s.v. 4. *es(s)* "a vessel".

12. iv. † †, **milk** (*lecna loim*), KM "bare flags". But the verse is talking about eatables, and the word *lom* "bare" would scarcely be used twice so close together; also, *leaca* is feminine; hence *loim* "a drop, milk", is preferable. For *lecna*, cf. *leacán* "wall-pennywort", *leacán* "sneezewort", Luibh.?

13. i. **produce of wild onions**, see ZCP, XVIII, 105, *mes melle*.

    iv. **crowberries** (*dercna froich*), KM "berries of the heath", but cf. Luibh., s.v. *dearc*.

15. i. **A cup † †, goodly hazlenuts** (*cuach comedh collain condla*), KM "a cup of mead of the hazlenut, bluebells". But "mead" is *midh*; some word beginning with *c*, for alliteration, is to be restored here (B). "Bluebells", KM, from Luibh., *coinnle corra* "bluebells"; but it is surely :*condail, cundail*, "good, virtuous, decent", etc.

    ii. **early young corn** (*condal ndaith*), KM "quick-growing rushes". *Condal* from *cannula*, "stalk, stubble, grass; *condal fand ferach*, YBL Corm. 944, young corn", S.

iii. oak-bushes (*durchain*); but cf. *darchán f.*, an acorn (O'Neachtan apud Dinneen)?

iv. †sweet-tangle† (*mertain*), so KM, from Luibh., *smeartan* "sweet tangle, sea-belt".

17. ii. a beloved movement (*forom ndil*), a cheville. *Forom* "movement" (S). The phrase occurs elsewhere as a cheville.

19. iii. speckled hooded birds (MS. *cochvill al-*), so B, reading *alaid* : *d*araigh. KM reads *alainn* "beautiful".

20. ii. the sea (MS. *cua-*); so B, reading *cuan* for rhyme with *ruad*. KM *cuach* "cuckoo".

22. ii. grey with cloud (*forglas neol*), B; KM "Upon the deep blue sky", but *nél* means "cloud" and is dative here; also, his translation seems to conflate *for glas* and *forglas*.

23. i. A beautiful pine (*caine ailme*), B, from *ailmm* a pine, gen. *ailmme*; lit. "beauty of a pine". KM "an excellent band", fr. *alma* "a herd", but the gen. sg. of this is *alma*.

iii. Though I sing (MS. *gec-*), so B, reading *ge can*. KM "ever young", fr. *gēcach* "branchy", etc., which does not give consonance and is difficult in meaning.

25. ii. which disturbs you (*immotoich*), so B, reading *immut-[f]oich*. KM "In my house", but this would be *im' thoich*.

VI

Attributed to Colum Cille. See pp. 109 and 93 note (1). Early twelfth century (GM). Ed. KM, ZCP v, 496; and MD, II, no. 42; tr. W. F. Skene, *Celtic Scotland* (Edinburgh, 1877), II, p. 92.

2. ii–iv. glittering…eternal, reading *luchair* and *suthain* with MD.

VII

See p. 93, note (2). Ed. Bruch. p. 60. No context.

VIII

See p. 93, note (2). Ninth century? Ed. Ir. T. III, p. 99, § 167; ed. and tr. Bruch. p. 66.

IX

See p. 93, note (2). Ninth century? Ed. Ir. T. III, p. 19, § 53. Ed. and tr. Bruch. p. 67.

X

See p. 93, note (2). Twelfth or thirteenth century (GM). Ed. and tr. Bruch. p. 66.

XI–XIII

See pp. 111–12, 119, 120, 122. Twelfth century (GM). From the Buile Shuibhne, ed. and tr. J. G. O'Keeffe, Irish Texts Society, vol. XII (1913), §§ 40, 45 and 58.

XI. 6. iii. **cress**, cf. Luibh., s.v. "watercress, salad".

XIII. 2. ii. **soft shoots**, *maothnatoin*; cf. O'Keeffe, *op. cit.*, glossary, and Irish poem XVII, 3, i, *maethain drissi dealgnaigi*.

4. iv. **wild onion** (*melle*), cf. ZCP, XVIII, 105.

XIV

See p. 117. Eighth century? From Cormac's Glossary, s.v. *ána* "a cup"; ed. KM, O. Bergin, R. I. Best, and J. G. O'Keeffe, *Anecdota from Irish MSS.*, IV (Halle, 1912), p. 5; tr. Stokes, *Sanas Cormaic*, s.v. *ána*. The place is Cnoc Raffonn in Tipperary. Fiacha, son of Eogan son of Oillil Óluim of Munster.

XV–XVIII

From the *Agallamh na Senórach*, written about A.D. 1200 (GM). Ed. O'Grady, *Silva Gadelica* (London, 1892), I, pp. 96, 102, 110 and 172; and tr. II, pp. 104, 109, 118, 192; ed. Stokes, Ir. T. IV, 1, pp. 3, 10, 21, 100.

XV. Caoilte describes the well of Tráigh Dhá Bhan, and goes on to tell how the members of the Fiana used to visit it (not given here). See p. 124.

3. iii. **arum lily**, see Ir. T. IV, 1, pp. 273, and 407, s.v. *gegar*.

XVI. Caoilte tells of the pleasures of the Isle of Arran. See p. 124. Ed. also MD, I, no. 40, from the Franciscan text of the Agallamh; tr. Anc. I. p. 59.

3. iii. **dense thorn-bushes in its**, reading *draighne dluithi ina* with the Franciscan MS. Book of Lismore, *dluith a fraigred re* "close are its dwellings to".

XVII. Caoilte describes a hill and the life of the Fiana there. See pp. 89, 123, and 125.

2. iv. **Cantyre.** Most of the places seem to be in W. Munster, but it is quite in keeping with the style of these poems for this to be the Cantyre in Scotland.

4. iii. **Berramain,** near Tralee (Stokes).

iv. **little nests.** Stokes suggests that these were to make the cooking fire with.

5. iv. **Deel,** a river rising in co. Cork and flowing into the Shannon.

6. iii. **meadhbhán,** "an esculent wild plant that causes intoxication", Dinneen. *Fáide,* now *Faoide* "Whiddy Island" (B).

XVIII. Caoilte (Oisín according to O'Rahilly, *op. cit.* p. 91) complains of the cold and tells how in his youth he regarded it with different feelings. See p. 116.

2. iii. **Echtge,** Slieve Aughty between Galway and Clare.

4. iii. **Tonn Tuaighe,** the Tuns, co. Antrim.

XIX

From the story of the Boromha; Finn and the Fiana are met by Molling Luath, one of Finn's foster-brothers, at the Point of Brocc Ross ("Badger Wood") on the Barrow, and he invites them to a feast and describes the food they shall have; the poem goes on to describe the rest of their entertainment (not given here). See p. 125. Twelfth century (GM). Ed. (as far as is given here) and tr. Stokes, RC, XIII, pp. 46–7; the whole poem is ed. (but not tr.) O'Grady, *Silva Gadelica,* II, pp. 364–5.

4. ii. Stokes prints ....*a Fid Daruba,* but there is no lacuna in the MS. or in the metre, though some article of food might have been expected. I take it with Lettir Faelchon. (O'Grady gives no gap.)

XX

Sliabh Cua, the Knockmealdown mountains. See p. 123, note (2). Ninth century? Ed. Ir. T. III, p. 87, § 99; ed. and tr. Bruch. p. 66.

XXI

Oisín tells St Patrick of the hill Benn Boilbin and its associations with the Fiana. See p. 89. Fifteenth or sixteenth century. From RIA MS., 12, I, 16, f. 43 ff. (A.D. 1814), which according to MD, I, pp. 89–90, was the ultimate source of the practically identical version in Hardiman's *Irish Minstrelsy* (London, 1831), II, 386. O'Rahilly, *op. cit.* no. 39, gives a very different version. The RIA text continues with a tale in verse about the Fiana.

1. iii. **son of Calpurnius**, i.e. St Patrick.
6. ii. **cuckoo-flower**, cf. Irish Texts Society, vol. XII, Glossary, s.v. *gleorán*.
7. There is one line too many here, and there must be some dislocation.

XXII

The sounds in which Finn delighted. See p. 87. Fifteenth or sixteenth century? Ed. *Transactions of the Ossianic Society*, IV, pp. 14–16. Also MD, I, no. 38 (somewhat different text).

1. ii. **Druim Dearg**, Drum Cliff, co. Sligo (O'Rahilly).
2. iii. **Maonmagh**, see poem V, 4, iv, note.
3. i. **Sliabh Crot**, one of the Galtees.
   ii. **Sliabh Cua**, see poem XX.
4. iii. **Bran**, Finn's favourite hound.

XXIII

Oisín praises the blackbird of Doire an Chairn and the sounds the Fiana loved. See p. 125. Fifteenth or sixteenth century? Ed. MD, I, no. 37.

1. i. **Doire an Chairn**, Derreenacarrin, in Beare (?) (O'Rahilly).
4. ii. **Druim Dá Loch**, Drumdallagh, Onom.
5. i. **Gleann Caoin**, Glenheen, co. Tipperary (O'Rahilly).

XXIV

See p. 89. Fourteenth century or later (GM). Ed. MD, II, no. 41. Note that the first line is the same as the opening line of Columba's Farewell (see p. 90).

2. iii–iv. A reference to the Pursuit of Diarmaid and Gráinne. **O'Duinn** = Diarmaid O'Duibhne.

XXV

See pp. 149, 160, 164, 169, 171, 173, 174. From "The Boyish Exploits of Finn", ed. KM, RC, v, pp. 201 ff.; ed. and tr. KM, *Four Songs*, pp. 8 ff.; tr. Anc. I. p. 54; dated by KM ninth or early tenth century. A difficult poem with many obscurities, written in a curious style (cf. *Four Songs*, Introd.). The poem is put into the story, which is much later and with which it has no real connection, as a composition of the boy Finn "to make trial of his poetic skill", after he had learned the art from Finn Éces; and it looks as if the compiler simply interpolated a poem believed to be the work of Finn to illustrate the tale of his apprenticeship to Finn Éces. There is nothing distinctively Fenian about the poem, and there would not be the slightest ground for supposing there were, but for the attribution.

2. i. **hardy** (*dean*), KM suggests *denn* to give rhyme with *fochen(n)*, and tr. "dust-coloured" (*denn* "dust, smoke"). But cf. Conts., s.v. *den*, which seems to mean "firm, strong, vigorous"; cf. *dron* used of birds in the next note. The internal rhyme is not to be pressed, as it is absent in some of the other verses.

iv. **the branching wood is a** † † **hedge** (*imme cerb caill craib*). *Cerb*? Cannot be *cerbb*, which is used of *caill*, a wood, and seems to have a meaning "sharp, prickly" (cf. Conts., s.v. *cerbb*, e.g. *gairid lon dron do chaill cheirp*, LL, 212; *canaid lon dron dord diambi forbb caill cerb*, rhyming with *bedc*, poem XVI, 6, i–ii), because of the rhyme *serb*; though that meaning would fit very well here.

3. ii. **water** (*linn*, i.e. *li(o)nn* rhyming with *fi(o)nn*), KM "pool", but this would be *linn* with slender *nn*.

4. i. A corrupt line. KM tries to extract a meaning, but it is not convincing.

9. i. †**black**† (*leig*), cf. *lattrach leig*, "†dark† puddle", poem XXIX, 3, i; and KM, *Über die Älteste Irische Dichtung* (Berlin, 1913–14), IV, v, 7, where *leig* is used of a king.

iv. **strong is the** † † (*is balc gedc*), KM "strong is the bound", but this is a guess; *gedg* (rhyming *bedg*) is unknown.

12. A difficult verse; the text is corrupt and something is lost; KM's attempt to restore it is unsatisfactory as his second line is still too short and does not rhyme with *geal*. I follow his restoration of line 1 and part of 2.

13. iii. **has been loosed** (*ro-saerad*), from *saerim* to liberate, free, deliver; so S, queried.

14. ii. **at the top of his voice** (*aird ucht*); the construction is not clear but the meaning seems plain.

XXVI

See pp. 149, 162, 164, 173. Tenth century (KM). Ed. and tr. KM, *Four Songs*, pp. 18 ff.; tr. Anc. I. p. 53.

This poem and no. XXIX are found in a short story in Rawlinson MS., B 502 f. 59 b, 2–f. 60 a, 1 (and in RIA, C III 2, f. 10 a), according to which Finn sent out a servant to fetch water who excused himself on the ground that the weather made it impossible, in poem XXIX; whereupon Finn replied that he was lying and sang this poem, "Summer has come", to refute him. The prose connecting the two tales is very exiguous, and is evidently a device to connect two independent poems attributed to the Fenians (cf. KM, RC, XI, p. 127). It is wholly incredible that even the laziest and most mendacious servant could be supposed to report weather like that of poem XXIX if it were actually the height of summer (and one would expect it to end "it is too cold to go out" instead of "so that none say anything but 'Cold'"), or that Finn, given the circumstances of poem XXIX, could have been so heartless a liar. This is made more certain by the fact that poem XXIX appears in LL, f. 208 a, by itself and without the story. Neither poem is in itself any more Fenian than the preceding, to which no. XXVI is strikingly similar in style (see KM, *Four Songs*, Introd.), and is of the same date, ninth or tenth century.

3. ii. active (*cass*), KM "curly", but cf. Conts., s.v. *cass* 2, which is a more probable meaning here.

7. ii. *Dedlaid lim fri sil snon*, KM "the brood of cares", but this is a guess, *snon* is unknown. (But RIA MS., C III 2, f. 10 a, reads *snō no son*, cf. O'Keeffe, *Buile Shuibhne*, § 36 note. This is the only important variant in this version.)

XXVII

See pp. 149, 171, 173. Ninth century. From the notes to the *Amra Choluim Cille*, where it is attributed to Finn; ed. and tr. Stokes, RC, XX, p. 258; ed. KM, *Four Songs*, p. 14, tr. Anc. I. p. 56. Here again there is no internal support for the attribution to Finn.

XXVIII

See p. 149. Ed. and tr. Bruch. p. 67.

XXIX

See pp. 162 and 173, and above on XXVI and below on XXX. Tenth century. Ed. and tr. KM, *Four Songs*, p. 18.

 3. i.   †dark† puddle, see note to XXV, 9, i.

  ii.   The idea seems to be that in common with the other objects mentioned the level land and the bogs have swelled, the one into raised ground (lit. "a standing-stone"), the other into a thick wood.

 4. ii.   **Colt's pillar**, presumably a standing-stone set up to one Colt.

XXX

See p. 173. Tenth century. Ed. and tr. KM, RC, XI, p. 125, with corrections in *Four Songs*, p. 16; tr. Anc. I. p. 57. This seems to belong better to its context than the preceding weather and seasonal poems; the story is that it was sung to Diarmaid and Gráinne by a treacherous old woman when they were hiding on the Hill of Howth, to prevent them going out and escaping Finn; verse 9, ll. i–ii, seem to fit this, but it may be an adaptation of a non-Fenian poem. It has a general resemblance to the preceding poem and no doubt belongs to the same group, but it can in no sense be regarded as a variant of it except in the case of verse 2, which is a variant of XXIX, 1. Still another version of this verse occurs in the LL copy of XXIX, and is perhaps the true one:

> Deathly cold!
> The storm has spread on every side;
> each gleaming furrow is a ford
> and every ford is a full mere.

It may have been attracted to XXX by the similarity of its first line to verse 1. i.

 1. ii.   **Magh Luirg**, in co. Roscommon.

 4. iii.   The idea is probably that the towns are flooded.

 6. ii.   **on the company of little birds** (*do menpaid na n-én*); *menpad* appears to be a collective (cf. "*menbach* = ? particles", S), "collection of small things"? rather than "small collection", as KM "little company of birds" takes it.

7. iv. up Benn Bó. The reading of the MS. *re pnnaib* implies *re pernaib*, "up the gaps" or "chasms", but it is difficult then to fit in *po*. KM reads *pennaib*, as tr. here (see *Four Songs*, p. 16).

8. i. eagle (*cuipiur*). Cormac's Glossary, *cupar*, i.e. *senén*, whence KM's "ancient bird"; but the word is evidently a generic term for birds of prey or carrion birds, cf. *cubhar* "an eagle", O'Clery; "a hawk", O'Reilly; "any carnivorous bird", Dinneen; "a bird of prey", Conts.; *cubhair*, i.e. *prechdin nó ilair*, ibid.

XXXI A–D

A few lines of prose tell how Athirne came on a visit to his foster-son Amorgein, and on wishing to depart next morning was detained by Amorgein with the first song; the process was repeated in winter and spring till Amorgein let him go with the fourth poem in summer. This is a most transparent device on the part of the compiler to explain and give a setting to four poems which must have existed before unattached, and there is nothing in them themselves to justify it, no mention of reasons for detaining Athirne, for example. Meyer's tr. of poem A. i, "a good stay-at-home season is autumn", begs the question. But the poems are obviously connected with each other in some way; see pp. 162, 163, 168, 172, 173.

MSS.: LL, f. 118 a; H 5280, f. 77 a (early sixteenth century), and RIA 23, N 10, ff. 15–16 (sixteenth century). Ed. and tr. KM, *Eriu*, VII, pp. 1 ff., from LL and H; the R text was printed by Thurneysen, *ibid.* pp. 196 ff. On the whole H and R agree against LL, and must be independent of it; the LL text is often corrupt, but so it seems was the original exemplar in places, and it is difficult to restore certain passages. Dated eleventh century by KM.

A. iv. hinds (LL *osseilt*, H *oselltae*, R *oisseillti*), see B.Dict., s.v. *elit*. KM "deer-herds", but the readings suggest *elit*, not *elta*.

v. shelter them (LL *ditnit*, H *dianit*, R *diánad*), with LL reading; but there is no object expressed and no alliteration with *oisseillti*, as there should be.

viii. high woods (*a ssithchailltib*), KM "long-leaved woods", which seems an unnatural and forced rendering.

xiii. **the hard ground is covered with heavy fruit.** I translate so, following a suggestion of Miss Knott's (made in conversation) that *lán* is to be taken as an adjective here, and *teinnithir*, the reading of R, =*teann*+*ithir*. LL *lan do mess trom tairnith-*, H ---*tindithir*, R ---*teinnithir*; KM "the weight of a heavy harvest bows them down", taking *tairnithir* from *do·airndim* "to let down"; but *lán* as a noun without a possessive is unusual, and if the verb is passive it is not clear what *lán* refers to.

B. ii. Reading *tuargabar* with LL; H *tuarcabann*, R *tuargab ann*, KM "the wave has raised up a heavy sea".

v. Lit. "except ravens of crimson blood".

c. ii. LL *uacht in gaeth gignither*, H --- *anagid*--, R -- *anagaidh*--, but alliteration with initial *g* is required; the LL line is a syllable too short; read *i ngaeth nglain* (B), or *ur-uacht*? KM reads *a n-agaid* and tr. "in the face", but the normal meaning of this phrase is "in opposition".

iv. A crux. LL *luind ic ecnacht corr cruadeigmi*, H *luind cennach corr cruadegme*, R *luind cendach corr cruadeigme*. The reading of LL suggests *luindiuc, luinneog, luinnéach*, "a chorus" etc.; cf. *luindec cuirri*, ZCP, III, 361, 11 (S); but *échnacht* is difficult. KM takes it as from *écndach* "reviling, blaspheming" (but also "lamenting", which would fit better here), and tr. "blasphemous chorus"; the meaning of *cennach* is unknown (it can hardly be *cennach* "a bargain" here), but the readings of H and R look like a compound of it with *laind* "eager, acrimonious, severe", and it is so taken here.

vii. Reading *eoin* with R. **islands**, LL *indferaid*, H *indseraid*, R *a hinnsenr-*. B suggests a collective *insenrad* from *inis*, with analogical *n* as in *giollanrad*.

D. i. LL *sithistar*, H *sithestar*, R *sitestar*; :*sioth* "peace"?

XXXII

Supposed to have been sung by Rumann mac Colmáin to the Vikings of Dublin in the eighth century (cf. KM, *Otia Merseiana*, II, pp. 76 ff.), but according to KM the poem is eleventh century. He bases this partly on the mention of the Sun-tree, deriving from the Alexander Saga which according to him was not known in Ireland till the eleventh century; but a verse of this poem is quoted in the Metrical Tract with forms older than the eleventh century.

See p. 91. Ed. and tr. KM, *Otia Merseiana*, II, pp. 76 ff.; tr. Anc. I. p. 51. KM, in his own copy of the Otia Merseiana text, kindly lent me by Professor Bergin, has made various marginal notes and some fresh readings of the MS.; these are referred to here as N.

1. i. **the plain of Ler**, i.e. the sea. Ler the sea-god, father of Manannán.

ii. MS. *-a- dana dar a hardimlibh*, but the line has seven syllables without the fragmentary word at the beginning.

iv. *Cu tet dar muir morga---*, Otia Merseiana; *morgasg-*, N; but this is an impossible form and would not rhyme.

v. *Rasfarraid g- garg-----*, Otia Merseiana, *ga garg --rid* N, so that the emendation *garg[g]emrid* is fairly certain. KM does not translate the line in Otia Merseiana; in Anc. I. he gives "it has pierced us like a spear", and in N, "the spear of the fierce winter season has pierced us" and "wintry weather has pierced us like a spear"; but *rasfarraid*, fr. *ro-fo-air-reth* with infixed pronoun, can only mean "has come upon" or "overtaken", and the infix is 3rd sg. fem. or 3rd pl. common, not 1st pl.; refers to *gaeth*?

4. ii–v. Meyer "It urges the dark fierce waves towards the southern world, surging in strife against the wide sky, listening to the witching song", Anc. I., a very free paraphrase. *Co mbad*, l. iii, is not the substantive, "that it should be (i.e. move) towards the southern world", but the copula, going closely with *ro-ferad* and *ra-ested*, "that it should be towards the southern world that it should make strife". *Fidnem*, Otia Merseiana "---sky", suggesting *findnem* "white sky"; but Anc. I. "wide sky", and N "arched" (? *fiodhbhac* "a bow"; but that is surely from *fiodh* "wood"?). *Delechduain*; Otia Merseiana, "I cannot translate *delech*"; Anc. I. and N "witching song"(?).

5. iv. *Co crann ngreine coresgeimh*. Coresgeimh? If the word is a compound, the g should be initial for alliteration, therefore *co res-geimh*; or *cores geimh, cuires geimh*, "that brings winter", but this is unlikely of the Sun-tree. *Geamh* "a branch"?

6. iii. **the island of Scit.** Skiddy Is., nr. Castlehaven (KM).

8. i. **a wild troubled sleep** (*suan garg sair*); *sáir* genitive sg. of *sár* "insult, outrage"?

iii–iv. MS. *fordath eala fortig mac Miled cona muintir*; KM "covers the sons of Mil with their people", reading *for[da]tig* as the line is a syllable short; but *mac* is acc. sg. or gen. pl., and in the phrase *mac Miled* is never singular when referring to the Irish; read *for a tig* (B), "(is) upon their house, (the house) of the sons of Miled with their people"?

v. **the wife of Manannán**, a kenning for the sea.

9. ii. **wide dark** (*íar-lethan*), so KM, Otia Merseiana and Anc. I., queried N. Cf. "*lugaid iardonn, .i. dubhdonn roboí*, CA, no. 23; but cf. *íar .i. folt*, Ir. T. III, 368, and *Feidhlimid íar glas .i. folt ghlas baí fair*, CA, no. 270" (S). So "wide-haired"?

v. **mountainous and raging**; MS. *sliabh dremon*, KM "Sliabh Dremon"; but the words must be a compound to rhyme with *iarlethan*, B.

XXXIII

Refers to the Viking raids on Ireland. See p. 91. Ninth century. Ed. and tr. Thes. Pal. II, 290; ed. Handbuch II, 39; tr. Anc. I. p. 101.

XXXIV

See p. 91. In the Annals: Annals of Ulster, s.a. A.D. 621 (see W. M. Hennessy, *Annals of Ulster*, Dublin, 1887, I, p. 92); Annals of Tigernach, see RC, XVII, p. 175. Ed. Pokorny, *An Early Irish Reader* (Halle, 1923), pp. 4–5; the translation given here is based on his text and notes. Early eighth century? (Pokorny). On the drowning of Conaing mac Aedain mac Gabrain.

2. i. **The woman**, a kenning for the sea.

iv. **Tree of Torta**, one of the five ancient trees of Ireland; the connection is not clear.

XXXV

See p. 91. Ninth century? Ed. Ir. T. III, 38, § 24; 102, § 187; ed. and tr. Bruch. p. 65.

XXXVI

See p. 85. Ed. and tr. Bruch. p. 67.

XXXVII

Ed. and tr. Ir. T. III, 67, § 2; Bruch. p. 67.

XXXVIII

On a place, Ceann Easgrach, or, "the crest of the ridge". Ed. Ir. T. III, p. 146, and KM, *Primer of Irish Metrics*, p. 15.
   iv. **of laths**, *do stiallchlethaib*, lit. "wattled strips".

XXXIX

Ed. Ir. T. III, 13, § 23; 42, § 48; ed. and tr. Bruch. p. 64.
   i. **Dairbre**, a place in Munster.
   ii. **young deer**, *ossoca* (for variants see Bruch. p. 64); "young deer, fawn", ? S.

XL

Ed. and tr. Bruch. p. 65.
   iv. Something is omitted in the MS.

XLI

Deirdre describes a glen. See p. 90. Fourteenth century or later (GM). Ed. MD, II, no. 43.
   6. ii. **active**, lit. "(leaping) like a goat", cf. O'Rahilly, *op. cit.*, Glossary, s.v. *bocach*.

THE WELSH POEMS

A

1. The beginning of summer, fairest season;
   noisy are the birds, green the woods,
   the ploughs are in the furrow, the ox at work,
   green the sea, the lands are many-coloured.

2. When the cuckoos sing in the tops of the fair trees
   my despondency becomes greater;
   the smoke is smarting, it is plain I cannot sleep.

3. Since my friends have passed away,
   in hill, in vale, in islands of the sea,
   in every way one goes,
   there is no seclusion from the blessed Christ.

B

1. Keen is the wind, bare the hill, it is difficult to find shelter,
   the ford is marred, the lake freezes,
   a man could stand on a single stalk.

2. Wave after wave covers the shore;
   very loud are the outcries before the heights of the hill;
   scarcely can one stand outside.

3. Cold is the bed of the lake before the tumult of winter,
   the reeds are withered, the stalks are broken,
   the wind is boisterous, the wood is †bare†.

4. Cold is the bed of the fish in the shelter of the ice,
thin is the stag, the grass is bearded,
short is the evening, the trees are bowed.

5. Snow falls, white is the surface;
warriors do not go on their business;
cold are the lakes, their colour is without warmth.

6. Snow falls, white is the hoarfrost;
idle is the shield on the shoulder of the aged;
very great is the wind, it freezes the grass.

7. Snow falls on the top of the ice,
the wind sweeps the crest of the close trees;
fine is a shield on the shoulder of the brave.

8. Snow falls, it covers the valley;
the warriors hasten to battle,
I do not go, a wound does not allow me.

9. Snow falls on the hillside,
the horse is a prisoner, the cattle are thin;
it is not like a summer day to-day.

10. Snow falls, white is the mountain-side,
bare are the timbers of the ship at sea;
a coward fosters many plans.

11. Gold rims about horns, †   † ,
cold are the paths, full of lightning the sky,
short is the evening, the tops of the trees are bent.

12. Bees in fodder, subdued is the clamour of birds,
the day is bleak....................
white-cloaked is the ridge of the hill, red the dawn.

13. Bees in cover; cold is the †surface† of the ford,
it freezes when there is frost;
in spite of all evasion death will come.

14. Bees in captivity; green is the sea;
    the reeds are withered, the slope is hard;
    cold and bleak is the world to-day.

15. Bees in shelter from the wet of winter;
    †   †, hollow is the cowparsnip;
    cowardice is an evil property in a man.

16. Long is the night, bare the moor, grey the slope,
    drab is the bank, the seagull is on the †hill†,
    rough are the seas; there will be rain to-day.

17. Dry is the wind, wet the path, brawling the watercourse,
    cold the groves, thin the stag;
    flood in the river; there will be fine weather.

18. Storm in the mountain, the rivers in turmoil,
    flood wets the level of the villages;
    the world is an ocean to look upon.

19. Thou art not a cleric, thou art not a †skulker†, oh chief;
    thou wilt not be called upon in the day of necessity;
    alas, Cyndilig, that thou wast not a woman!

20. The bent deer makes for the end of the sheltered coombe;
    the ice breaks, the lands are bare;
    a brave man can escape from many a strait.

21. The thrush is spotted-breasted,
    spotted is the breast of the thrush;
    the edge of the bank breaks under the hoof of the thin bent crooked deer;
    very noisy is the loud-shouting wind,
    scarcely in truth can one stand outside.

22. Winter's Day; dusky, dark and matted, is the top of the heather,
foaming is the wave of the sea;
short is the day; let your counsel be fulfilled.

23. With the protection of a shield and the vigour of a steed
and brave-fearless men,
fine is the night to rout the enemy.

24. Swift is the wind, raw and bare the wood,
the reeds are withered, the deer is hardy;
wicked Pelis, what land is this?

* * * * * * *

35. Men in battle; the ford is freezing,
chilly is the wave, many-coloured the breast of the sea;
may the Lord give us deep counsel.

* * * * * * *

C

1. It is my heart's desire to sit upon the hill
and yet it does not rouse me;
short is my course, deserted is my homestead.

2. Keen is the wind, †bare   cattle†,
when the wood puts on the fair colours of summer
very ill am I to-day.

3. I am not †active†, I do not keep retainers,
I cannot move about;
as long as it lists it let the cuckoo sing.

4. The loquacious cuckoo sings with the day
a †loud† song in the meadows of Cuawg;
better is the spendthrift than the miser.

5. In Aber Cuawg sing the cuckoos
   on the flowery branches;
   long let the loquacious cuckoo sing.

6. In Aber Cuawg sing the cuckoos
   on the flowery branches;
   woe to the sick man who hears them perpetually.

7. In Aber Cuawg the cuckoos sing;
   it grieves my heart
   that one who has heard them will not hear them again.

8. I have listened to the cuckoo on the ivy-tree;
   my shield has become weak;
   the sense of loss for what I loved is greater.

9. I listened to the note of the birds
   in the crest of the †rustling† oak;
   loud cuckoo, everyone remembers what he loves.

10. The songster of perpetual song, plaintive is its note,
    of roving course, with the flight of a hawk,
    the voluble cuckoo in Aber Cuawg.

11. Clamorous are the birds, damp the glens,
    the moon shines, cold is the midnight hour;
    sore is my heart with the affliction of melancholy.

12. Bright are the tops of the glens, long is the midnight hour;
    the skilful are honoured;
    I have a right to the grant of sleep for old age.

13. Clamorous are the birds, wet is the shingle,
    the leaves fall, sad is the exile;
    I do not deny, I am sick to-night.

14. Clamorous are the birds, wet is the strand,
    bright the firmament, broad the wave;
    the heart is withered with longing.

15. Clamorous are the birds, wet is the strand,
    bright is the wave of broad course;
    my youth †is gone†—
    I would I might get it back.

16. Clamorous are the birds on the height of Edrywy;
    loud the cry of hounds in the waste;
    clamorous the birds again.

17. The beginning of summer, pleasant is every †growth†;
    when warriors hasten to battle
    I do not go, a wound does not allow me.

18. The beginning of summer, it is pleasant on the bank;
    when warriors hasten to the battle-field
    I do not go, a wound burns me.

19. Grey is the crest of the mountain, fragile the tops of the ash trees,
    the shining wave ebbs from the river-mouths;
    laughter is far from my heart.

20. It is to-day the end of a month
    that I have been in the dwelling that he has left;
    sore is my heart, fever has laid hold on me.

21. Clear is the sight of the watchman;
    idleness makes for arrogance;
    sore is my heart, disease wastes me.

22. The cattle are in the shed, the mead in the vessel;
    the prosperous man does not desire discord;
    patience is the outline of understanding.

23. The cattle are in the shed, the beer in the vessel;
    slippery are the paths, †violent† is the shower,
    and deep is the ford. The heart concocts treason.

24. Treachery concocts a wicked deed—
    there will be suffering when it is atoned—
    a selling of little for much.

25. †   †;
    when the Lord judges throughout the long day
    dark will be falsehood, bright the truth.

26. †   †;
    men are merry over the ale;
    withered are the reeds, the cattle are in the shed.

27. I have heard the wave of heavy roar
    loud among the shingle and the pebbles;
    sore is my heart with depression to-night.

28. Branching are the tops of the oaks, bitter the taste o
        the ash,
    sweet is the cowparsnip, laughing the wave;
    the cheek does not hide the affliction of the heart.

29. Frequent is the sighing that †comes upon me†
    after my wont;
    God does not allow good to the perverse.

30. Good is not allowed to the perverse,
    but grief and anxiety;
    God does not undo what he has done.

31. The leper was a youth, he was a resolute chief
    in the court of a king;
    may God be kind to the outcast.

32. What is done in an †oratory†,
    wicked is he who reads it;
    what man hates here God hates above.

D

1. †Serried is the host, budding the ash;†
   the ducks are in the lake, white-pebbled is the wave;
   stronger than a hundred is the counsel of the heart.

2. Long is the night, sad the salt-marsh;
   usual is commotion in an assembly;
   the mischievous and the good do not agree.

3. Long is the night, sad the mountain;
   the wind whistles over the top of the trees;
   an ill-disposition does not lead the righteous astray.

4. The saplings of the green-crested birch
   draw my foot from the fastening;
   do not confess your secret to a youth.

5. The saplings of the oak-trees in the grove
   draw my foot from the chain;
   do not confess a secret to a maid.

6. The saplings of the leafy oak
   draw my foot from the fetters;
   do not confess a secret to a babbler.

7. The saplings of bramble with berries on it;
   neither a blackbird on its nest
   nor a liar are ever silent.

8. Rain outside, it wets the fern,
   white is the shingle of the sea, the shore is foamy;
   understanding is a fair candle for man.

9. Rain outside of the shelter;
   yellow is the gorse, withered the cowparsnip;
   Lord God, why hast thou made a coward?

10. Rain outside, it wets my hair;
    querulous is the feeble, precipitous the cliff,
    grey the ocean, salt the brine.

11. Rain outside, it wets the deep;
    the wind whistles over the top of the reeds;
    every achievement is lacking without its talent.

E

1. Mountain snow, white is every place;
   the raven is accustomed to sing;
   good does not come of excessive sleeping.

2. Mountain snow, white is the ravine,
   the trees bend at the assault of the wind;
   many a couple love each other
   but never come together.

3. Mountain snow, the wind heaps it;
   broad is the full moon, green the dock-leaves;
   a mischievous man is rarely without litigation.

4. Mountain snow, swift is the stag;
   usual are valiant chieftains in Britain;
   there is need of discretion for the alien.

5. Mountain snow, the stag in heat,
   ducks in the pond, white is the ocean;
   slow is the old man, easy to overtake him.

6. Mountain snow, the stag is roaming;
   the heart smiles on what it loves;
   though a tale be told me
   I recognise what is shameful wherever it be.

7. Mountain snow; white pebbled is the shingle;
   the fish is in the ford; one is sheltered in a cave;
   hateful is he who oppresses.

8. Mountain snow, the stag in flight;
usual for a chieftain to have a splendid weapon
and to mount by the side of the saddle-pommel
†and   †.

9. Mountain snow, the stag is hunched;
much have I said indeed;
this is not like a summer day.

10. Mountain snow, the stag is hunted;
the wind whistles over the eaves of the tower;
grievous, my friend, is sin.

11. Mountain snow, the stag is leaping;
the wind whistles over the high white wall;
it is usual for the calm to be comely.

12. Mountain snow, the stag is in the vale;
the wind whistles over the top of the roof;
evil does not conceal itself wherever it be.

13. Mountain snow, the stag is on the strand;
the old man misses his youth;
an ill countenance hampers a man.

14. Mountain snow, the stag is in the grove;
very black is the raven, swift the roebuck;
the healthy and free, it is strange that he complains.

15. Mountain snow, the stag is in the rushes,
cold are the bogs; mead is in the vat;
usual for the wounded is lamentation.

16. Mountain snow, flecked is the front of the tower,
the animals make for shelter;
woe to the woman who gets a bad husband.

17. Mountain snow, flecked is the front of the crag,
withered the reeds, the cattle †shun the water†;
woe to the man who gets a bad wife.

18. Mountain snow, the stag is in the ditch,
    the bees sleep snugly;
    well agreed are the thief and long night.

19. Mountain snow; liverwort in the river;
    slow to strife
    the sluggard does not soon avenge an insult.

20. Mountain snow; there are fish in the lake;
    proud is the hawk, curly-haired are chiefs;
    everyone does not get what he wants.

21. Mountain snow; the crest of the †pear tree† is brown;
    fierce and serried are spears;
    alas, for longing, my brothers.

22. Mountain snow; swift is the wolf,
    it frequents the border of the wilderness;
    usual is every hurt upon †the wretched†.

23. Mountain snow, the stag is not slow;
    rain falls from the sky;
    sadness breeds utter despondence.

24. Mountain snow, the deer are nimble;
    the waves wet the brink of the strand;
    the skilful, let him conceal his design.

25. Mountain snow, the stag is in the glen;
    summer is calm, the lake is still;
    greybearded is the ice; the brave is on the exposed side.

26. Mountain snow; speckled is the breast of the goose;
    strong is my arm and my shoulder,
    I pray I may not be a hundred years old.

27. Mountain snow, bare are the tops of the reeds,
    Bent the tops of the branches; there are fish in the ocean;
    where there is no learning there will be no mental facility.

28. Mountain snow, there are fish in the ford,
the thin bent stag makes for the sheltered coombe;
longing for the dead does not avail.

29. Mountain snow, the stag is in the wood;
the fortunate does not journey on foot;
the coward fosters many hurts.

30. Mountain snow, the stag is on the hillside;
the wind whistles over the top of the ash-trees;
a third foot to the aged is his stick.

31. Mountain snow, the stag is swimming;
ducks in the lake; white is the lily;
the perverse is not willing to listen.

32. Mountain snow; red are the feet of hens;
water is shallow where it babbles,
talking big increases the disgrace.

33. Mountain snow, the stag is swift;
scarcely anything at all interests me;
warning avails nothing to the unfortunate.

34. Mountain snow, white is its fleece;
rarely is the face of a friend kindly
at frequent visiting.

35. Mountain snow, white are the roofs of houses;
if the tongue related what the mind knew,
none would be neighbours.

36. Mountain snow, day has come;
sick are the sad, bare the ill-clad;
usual is every hurt for the fool.

F

1. Usual is wind from the south; usual a deposit in a church;
   usual for a weak man to be thin;
   usual for a person to ask for news;
   usual for a foster-child to have luxuries.

2. Usual is wind from the east; usual for a portly person to be pompous;
   usual a blackbird among thorns;
   usual after great violence is great lamentation;
   usual for ravens to get flesh in a wood.

3. Usual is wind from the north; usual for maids to be sweet;
   usual is a handsome man in Gwynedd;
   usual for a prince to provide a feast;
   usual is despondency after drinking.

4. Usual is wind from the sea; usual the surge of flood-tide;
   usual for a pig to breed swine-lice;
   usual for swine to root up earth-nuts.

5. Usual is wind from the mountain; usual is a dullard in the country;
   usual to get thatching in marshes;
   usual for a cleric to be reared on milk;
   usual are leaves and saplings and trees.

6. Usual from bastardy for men to be base
   and for bad women to be feasted on mead,
   and distress to be on the grandson, and the great-grandson to be worse and worse.

7. Usual is an eagle's nest in the top of an oak,
   and talkative men in the tavern;
   gentle is the look on whom one loves.

8. Usual is a day †with a blazing fire† in the †damp† of winter;
   chieftains are †free of speech†;
   usual for the hearth of the irreligious to be deserted.

9. Withered are the stalks, and flood is in the brook;
   the Englishman traffics in money;
   loveless is the heart of the mother of false children.

10. This leaf which the wind drives,
    woe to it for its fate!
    Old it is, this year it was born.

11. Though it be small, ingenious
    is the nest of the birds in the border of the wood;
    the good and the fortunate will live to a like age.

12. Cold and wet is the mountain, cold and grey the ice;
    trust in God will not deceive you;
    long consideration prevents long tribulation.

G

1. Winter's Day,[1] hard are the berries,
   leaves aloft, the pond is full;
   the morning before his going
   woe to him who trusts a stranger.

2. Winter's Day; fine is a secret shared;
   the wind is as swift as a storm;
   it is the work of a skilful man to hide a secret.

[1] I.e. the first of November, see note.

3. Winter's Day, thin are the stags,
   yellow are the tops of the birches, the summer steading
       is deserted;
   woe to him who incurs shame for a trifle.

4. Winter's Day, bent are the tops of the branches;
   usual is commotion from the mouth of the mischievous;
   where there is no natural gift there will be no learning.

5. Winter's Day, rough is the weather,
   unlike early summer;
   there is no diviner but God.

6. Winter's Day; sweet-songed are the birds;
   short is the day; loud are the cuckoos;
   the merciful providence of God is best.

7. Winter's Day; what is parched is hard;
   very black is the raven, swift is the sturdy;
   the youth laughs when the old man stumbles.

8. Winter's Day, thin are the stags;
   woe to the weak when he is angry; ephemeral will be
       the world;
   true, better is kindliness than comeliness.

9. Winter's Day, bare is the burning,
   the plough is in the furrow, the ox at work;
   from a hundred scarcely a friend.

H

1. Delightful are the tops of the ash-trees, tall and bright
       are they
   when they grow at the head of the glens;
   a heart full of longing leads to sickness.

2. Delightful are the tops of the glens; long is the hour of midnight;
the skilful are honoured;
a maiden owes the grant of repose to sickness.

3. Delightful are the tops of the willows, †brisk† is the fish in the lake;
the wind whistles over the tops of the small branches;
nature is stronger than precept.

4. Delightful is the top of the gorse and a secret shared with the wise,
but a fool is boorish;
there is no diviner but God.

5. Delightful are the tops of the clover-flowers; dispirited is the coward;
weary are the jealous;
usual for the weak are anxieties.

6. Delightful are the tops of the reeds; wrathful are the jealous;
it is rarely one can do it—
it is the part of the discerning man to love truly.

7. Delightful are the tops of the mountains; at the disturbance of winter
withered are the reeds; †a prudent aspect† is serious;
there is no modesty in hunger.

8. Delightful are the tops of the mountains; mighty is the cold of winter;
the reeds are withered; there is froth on mead;
want †befalls† in exile.

9. Delightful are the tops of the oak-trees; bitter are the twigs of ash-trees;
before the ducks the wave breaks;
thought is valiant; care has been long in my heart.

10. Delightful are the tops of the oak-trees; bitter are the twigs of ash-trees;
    sweet is the cowparsnip; laughing is the wave;
    the cheek does not hide the affliction of the heart.

11. Delightful are the tops of the wild rose berries; there is no formality in hardship;
    let each guard what he prizes;
    the worst blemish is bad manners.

12. Delightful is the top of the broom, a trysting-place for lovers,
    very yellow are the clustering branches;
    the ford is shallow; it is usual for the contented to be drowsy.

13. Delightful is the top of the apple-tree; very wise are the fortunate;
    †   †
    and after loving leaving in want.

14. Delightful is the top of the apple-tree; very wise are the fortunate;
    long is the day; the dullard is depraved;
    there is frost at dawn; the blind man is a prisoner.

15. Delightful is the top of the hazel by the hill of Digoll;
    care-free are the empty-headed;
    it is the part of the powerful to keep his pledge.

16. Delightful are the tops of the reeds; usual for the dullard to be sluggish,
    and for the youth to be a pupil;
    none but a fool breaks his promise.

17. Delightful is the top of the iris; the reckless are wine-bibbers;
    the word of a retinue is reliable,
    usual for the faithless to break his word.

J

1. There is cackling from the hen; there is clamour from the brave,
   there is care upon the one who loves him;
   the heart is broken with grief.

2. Loud-laughing is the deaf; the rash is fickle;
   the mischievous is quarrelsome;
   happy is he on whom looks one who loves him.

3. The priest is trustworthy; the horse is a trotter;
   the student is greedy;
   the liar is deceitful.

4. The knight is conspicuous, the thief is skulking;
   a woman deceives a rich man;
   a lazy shepherd is the friend of the wolf.

5. The sea is green, the wave is glad;
   mournful are the sick,
   sad are the old and ill.

6. The furrow is wet; surety is frequent;
   the pet-dog is snarly, the old woman is spiteful;
   the sick is querulous, the healthy is joyful.

7. The pet-dog is snarly, the snake is poisonous;
   the ford is waded with the help of staves;
   the †adulterer† is no better than the thief.

8. The perverse is disagreeable; the young are wild;
   old age leads to poverty;
   there are pleasant men at a mead-feast.

9. The lake is deep; spears are keen;
   the brave is a dependable lion in battle;
   the prosperous is wise, God protects him.

10. The swineherds are glad (when) the wind rises;
the fortunate is his own protection,
usual is disaster for the mischievous.

11. The beadle is fond of accusing; the goose is quarrelsome;
the welcome goes with the clothes;
the bard is beloved by the generous.

12. The seagull is white, the wave is loud;
blood is staining on the ashen spear;
frost is grey; the heart is bold.

13. Bold is the chief and avid of heart,
and he is a spearman in defence;
he who does not give does not keep his honour.

14. The furze is sharp, and the exile is an outcast;
the fatuous is apt to laugh;
the moor is bare; the leek is pungent.

K

1. The month of January, the valley is smoky,
the cup-bearer is weary, the wandering bard is in distress,
the raven is thin, the hum of bees is rare,
the byre is empty, the kiln is cold;
degraded is the man who is not worthy to be asked for anything;
woe to him who loves his three enemies;
Cynfelyn spoke truth:
"The best candle for man is good sense."

2. The month of February, a feast is rare,
the spade and the wheel are hard at work,
usual is disgrace out of frequent imputation;

woe to him who makes needless accusation;
three things which turn into evil poison—
a woman's advice, murder, and conspiracy;
†a rainbow on a spring morning;†
woe to him who strikes his maidservant;
the evening is good for enjoyment.

3. The month of March, great is the pride of birds,
bitter is the cold wind over the end of the ploughed field;
good weather is longer than crops,
anger lasts longer than sorrow;
every creature dreads its enemy,
every bird knows its mate;
everything arises out of the earth
except the dead, great is his prison!

4. The month of April, the upland is misty,
the oxen are weary, the earth is bare,
feeble is the stag, playful the long-eared (hare);
usual is a guest though he be not invited;
everyone has many faults where he is not loved;
blessed is he who is faithful;
usual is destruction upon the children of the wicked;
usual after arrogance is lasting death.

5. The month of May, the ploughman is extravagant;
every dyke is shelter to the destitute;
joyful is the lightly clad old man;
the wood is leafy, the wanton is glad;
reconciliation is easy where there is love;
tuneful are the cuckoo and the hound;
not less soon in going to market
is the lamb's skin than the sheep's skin.

6. The month of June, beautiful are the lands,
   the sea is smooth, the strands are gay,
   long and fair is the day, women are lively,
   the flock is abundant, the bogs are passable;
   God loves all peace,
   the devil causes all mischief;
   everyone desires honour;
   the strong comes to a feeble end.

7. The month of July, the hay is under cover,
   the sunshine is hot, the hailstones melt;
   the robber likes not a long truce;
   the seed of an unchaste body does not prosper;
   shame completely avenges a boast;
   the rickyard is full, the † † fair is half empty;
   the foster son of Mary spoke truth—
   "God judges, man talks."

8. The month of August, the salt-marsh is †full of snails†,
   the bees are merry, the hive is full;
   the work of the sickle is better than that of the bow;
   the rick is more frequent than the playing-field;
   who works not nor prays,
   he does not deserve his bread;
   Saint Brenda spoke truth—
   "Evil is sought after no less than the good."

9. The month of September, there is verse in the Canon,
   the ripening season of corn and fruit;
   woe to my heart for longing;
   the eye of God is upon the poor;
   the worst privilege is the insulting of people,
   the worst good is through perjury;
   arrogance and oppression of the innocent
   are the ruin of heirs.

10. The month of October, the axle is hard worn,
the stag is wanton, the wind is swift;
usual are plunderers in war;
usual for theft to become manifest;
woe to the mischievous who cares not what he does;
it is not easy to escape disaster;
death is certain for all,
uncertain is the day when it will come.

11. The month of November, the fool grumbles,
the wethers are fat, the woods are half-bare;
the time that comes with joy,
a time of sadness will outbalance it;
wealth is not the property of the miser,
it is the generous one who gives it away who shall
    possess it;
man and the goods of the world will pass away,
but the goods of Heaven will be everlasting.

12. The month of December, of short days and long nights,
there are ravens among the young plants, rushes on
    the moor,
the bee and the nightingale are silent;
there is conflict at the end of a night's carousal;
the house of the fortunate is sound;
the mischievous does harm without cause;
life, in spite of the length of its sojourn,
will pass away in a day and a night.

NOTES

A

See pp. 114, 149, 179–180. Twelfth century? Ed. and annotated H. Lewis, *Hen Gerddi Crefyddol*, pp. 5 and 118. It is treated in the manuscript (BBC) as part of the poem *Moli Duu in nechrev a diuet* (f. xv ff.), but Lewis makes a separate poem of it in rather irregular englynion; this is not certain.

St. 2, l. iii, i.e. the speaker cannot sleep for longing for his friends; the remark about the smoke is obscure, unless it is an apology for his sleepless and tear-reddened eyes.

B

See pp. 149, 177–8, 184, 189 note 1. Tenth or eleventh century? Edition and notes, EWGP, pp. 18 ff. and 43 ff.

St. 1, l. iii, i.e. because the grass is frozen so hard.

C

See p. 114 and *ibid*. notes 2 and 3. Tenth or eleventh century? Ed. and notes, CLH, pp. 23 ff. and 160 ff.

St. 32, ll. ii–iii, i.e. the penitent reading penance in an oratory.

D–I

Early twelfth century? Ed. and notes, EWGP, pp. 20 ff. and 46 ff.

G, st. 1, l. i, **Winter's Day**, i.e. November 1st, the beginning of the Celtic winter.

J

On the MSS., see EWGP, pp. 9 ff.; and for text and notes, *ibid*. pp. 35 ff. and 65 ff. Early twelfth century?

K

"The Verses of the Months." On the MSS., see EWGP, pp. 12 ff., and for text and notes, *ibid*. pp. 37 ff. and 65 ff. Last half of the fifteenth century?

Part Two
STUDIES ON THE POEMS

INTRODUCTION

"Die keltische Poesie können wir vielleicht am besten mit einem einzigen Worte charakterisieren; sie ist unendlich primitiv."[1]

What does "infinitely primitive" really mean, of poetry? Professor Sieper does not tell us; but primitive poetry may be defined as an expression in crude verse form, without conscious literary art, of the singer's own immediate needs in an uncultured stage of society. Primitive nature poetry consists in practice usually of hymns to nature divinities, charms, occupational songs, fertility chants, and prophecies, songs describing an animal hunted, seasonal carols, and so on; it is not interested in the poetic aspects of nature for their own sake and does not seek closely in it for anything with a more than utilitarian bearing on human affairs. The Irish and Welsh poets of the early Middle Ages were not aboriginal savages, nor were they peasants chanting fertility carols from door to door; and one is at a loss to understand how a poem like no. II or no. XVI can be called "infinitely primitive". Perhaps Sieper meant "simple", or "sincere", "not artificial". This would apply well enough to most (not all) of the nature poems with which we are concerned, but there is a great deal in "die keltische Poesie" which is highly artificial. Poems so delightfully simple as our nature songs are not always the rule.

The same author declares further:

Wohl finden wir auch in den alten Literaturen anderer Völker Liebe und Verständnis für die Schönheit der Natur, aber nirgends, ausser der Dichtung der Kelten (oder wo ihr Einfluss offenbar ist) finden wir eine Dichtkunst die sich mit der Natur nur um ihrer selbst willen beschäftigt.[2]

[1] E. Sieper, *Die Altenglische Elegie*, p. 65. [2] *Ibid.*

That is, that Celtic nature poetry is interested in nature objectively and for its own sake alone, not subjectively for its relation to the poet's own, more important, feelings. If this were true, it is not a primitive characteristic. Nature for its own sake is not generally a subject of interest until a comparatively late date in the growth of culture, as is well known to be the case with Greek literature.[1] In fact, it is only very partially true of early Irish and Welsh poetry. Some groups do deal with nature in an objective way, but this is due to certain special causes; Welsh nature-gnomic poetry is entirely objective, since classification and description is its very purpose (see p. 135), and the seasonal poems (Chapter IV) which are concerned only to detail the signs and characteristics of a season have very little room for the poet's own explicit feelings about the matter. But the hermit poems and the elegies and early Fenian poems, the best in early Celtic nature poetry, are concerned most vitally with the singer's own reactions to his surroundings; not with making a descriptive catalogue about the various things he sees, but with telling us how he feels about them and how they harmonise or clash with his own particular mood. Whoever has sat with a book in the woods in April will understand what the poet of no. II was feeling as he wrote in his "lined little booklet". "Pleasant is the glittering of the sun to-day upon these margins because it flickers so", was what an Irishman scribbled one idle moment in the margin of his volume of Cassiodorus: and Dr Flower remarks "It is the emotion, not the sun, that matters here."[2] So in the best of Irish and Welsh nature poetry, it is the emotion, not the sun, that matters.

[1] Cf. E. E. Sikes, *Roman Poetry* (Methuen, 1923), p. 108.
[2] "Religion and Literature in Ireland in the VIIIth and IXth Centuries", *Report of the Church of Ireland Conference for* 1932 (Dublin, 1932), p. 73.

I should like to apply a new adjective to Celtic nature poetry at its best—not "primitive" nor "objective", nor yet "magical" and "romantic", as some who knew nothing about it have declared; but "imaginative". This does not mean "romantic" or "false", though the word is frequently used in those senses in English, but "vitally felt and expressed with emotional insight". The contrast between the imaginative and the unimaginative treatment may be illustrated from two late Latin poems, the *Pervigilium Veneris* and a well-known passage of Tiberianus. Contrast this description of dewdrops on buds from the *Pervigilium*:

> *Emicant lacrimae trementes de caduco pondere,*
> *gutta praeceps orbe parvo sustinet casus suos;*
> *umor ille quem serenis astra rorant noctibus*
> *mane virgines papillas solvit umenti peplo,*

with this passage from Tiberianus:

> *Subtus autem molle gramen flore pulchro creverat,*
> *tum croco solum rubebat et lucebat liliis....*
> *Has per umbras omnis ales, plus canora quam putes,*
> *cantibus vernis strepebat et susurris dulcibus,*

and the dreadful banality of

> *sic euntem per virecta pulchra odora et musica*
> *ales, amnis, aura, lucus, flos, et umbra, iuverat,*

and the distinction between the imaginative and the unimaginative treatment of nature will be clear. The one makes the thoughts vividly alive with a shock of delight at its *lacrimae trementes de caduco pondere*; and the other is a dull catalogue of all the things which the poet felt proper to a river valley, seen without imagination and expressed in conventional phrases drawn from generations of preceding Latin poets—*molle gramen, flore pulchro, susurris dulcibus* and the "incredibly melodious" birds.[1] Certainly, the unimaginative treatment is sometimes found in Irish nature poetry, but for the most part its real value, which distinguishes it from not a little Classical nature poetry and from almost all that of the Middle Ages, lies not in its being "infinitely primitive" nor in describing nature for its own sake, but in possessing to a remarkable degree this power of imaginative treatment.

Our early Celtic nature poetry is the work of literary artists, not the crude chant of primitive man; but many a literary genre has arisen from expressions of thought that are more primitive, and it is instructive to analyse the more notable ways in which nature poetry has come into being as literature in other languages, and to see how and why some of them appear in Irish and Welsh and some do not.

An important group in the Celtic poetry is that based on observations of the seasons and of the signs that precede them, and the songs that are sung at their festivals; and the weather, in the form of prognostications, prophecies of fertility, and actual weather descriptions.[2] This group will be discussed in Chapter IV and need only be mentioned here.

A source of nature poetry in many languages is the hymn to nature divinities in which their particular natural associations are described. It is found in the Vedic Hymns; for example in that to Ratri, the Night:

The goddess Night coming on has looked out in many places with her eyes; she has assumed all glories....

---

[1] The *Pervigilium* has often been ascribed to Tiberianus on grounds of style, which in view of the above note seems exceedingly improbable to the writer.

[2] And on times of day; cf. Theocritus, VII, 21–23: "Simichidas, where are you going now at midday, when even the lizard sleeps in the hedgerow and the crested larks do not stray abroad?"

So to-day to us, at her coming we have gone home like birds to their nest on the tree.

The peasants have gone home, and footed creatures and winged creatures, even the voracious hawks....

Darkness has come upon me, painting, black, palpable; wipe it out, Dawn, like a debt.[1]

The Homeric Hymns have several passages of this kind; the hymn to Pan begins:

Tell me, Muse, of the dear son of Hermes, the goat-footed, the two-horned, the lover of clatter, who roams about the woody glens with the dance-loving nymphs who tread the crests of some sheer crag, calling upon Pan....

And the Hymn to Artemis (ll. 4–9):

(Artemis) who about the shadowy mountains and windy crags draws her bows of gold, joying in the chase, and sends forth her grievous arrows; and the crests of the lofty mountains tremble, and the thick wood rings terribly in response at the screaming of the wild beasts, and the earth shudders and the fishy sea.

Nature hymns are not found in the early literatures of the British Isles, since if they ever existed they were extinguished before the literary period by the coming of Christianity. The Irish otherworld poems have a certain likeness however in being descriptions, not of the gods and their attributes themselves, but of their home or the home of the dead. The Voyage of Bran is the best of several examples, with parallels in Greek, Anglo-Saxon, and elsewhere.[2] Actually descriptions of nature in the Voyage of Bran are not developed enough for it to be called a nature poem.

---

[1] See A. A. Macdonell, *A Vedic Reader for Students* (2nd ed., Oxford, 1928), pp. 203 ff. Cf. a Sumerian hymn to the sun, tr. Z. A. Ragozin, *The Story of the Nations* (Fisher Unwin, 1889), vol. II (Chaldea), pp. 171–2.

[2] See K. Meyer and A. Nutt, *The Voyage of Bran*. An example in Mediaeval Latin, with the usual features, is the picture of the abode of Cupid in the poem "De Phyllide et Flora", *Carmina Burana*, p. 155.

Nature descriptions are common in similes, but they demand a considerable sensibility to nature to make the comparison possible, and consequently are little used in literatures where nature is not a matter of some interest. The Homeric similes show this sensibility highly developed, but the early poetry of Western Europe much less so. Similes are rather rare in Anglo-Saxon,[1] and rarer still in Norse. Two similes are quoted by Professor and Mrs Chadwick from the Hamthismál and the Guthrunarkvitha, I:[2] "I am left in solitude like an aspen in a wood, bereaved of kinsfolk like a fir of its branches, robbed of pleasure like a tree of its foliage, when the 'branch-destroying' comes on a warm day"; and "In comparison with the sons of Gjúki my Sigurthr was like a garlic standing out above the grass, or a bright stone, a precious stone, set in a collar worn by a prince". Similes are not over-common in Irish and Welsh, except where in love poetry women are compared with various natural objects. A Welsh simile which is of the same type as the two Norse examples quoted occurs in the Cynddylan elegy of the Red Book of Hergest, col. 1048, ll. 5–6: "I have had brothers who were not evil, who grew up like hazel saplings; one by one they have all passed away". It will be noticed that this and the two Norse similes are all from elegies on the dead, where comparisons like these would be natural. The same figure as in this Welsh passage is found in Sappho, ὄρπακι βραδίνω σε μάλιστ' ἐικάσδω, "I liken thee most of all to a slender sapling", though this is from a love poem, not an elegy. Professor Gwynn Jones has collected a list of similes from the love

[1] E.g. the similes from seafaring in the *Crist*, ll. 851 ff. (Grein-Wülcker, *Bibliothek*, III, 1, pp. 1 ff.): "Now it is most like as if we were sailing in boats on the flood over the cold water, conveying our sea-timbers across the wide sea in our ocean steeds."

[2] H. M. and N. K. Chadwick, *The Growth of Literature*, vol. I, pp. 515 and 512.

poetry of the Welsh bardic poets;[1] for example *hoen gynwaneg maen pan wisg ton frwysgflaen gaen am garreg*, "of the colour of a rock among the billows when the impetuous-fronted wave folds its surface about the stone"; *hoen geirw man*, "of the hue of small ripples"; *blawd blaen afallgyr*, "like the blossom on the crest of an apple bough". In Irish, the quatrain no. XXXVI, of unknown context, has a remarkable and unusual simile about the wind, and there is a series of similes in the poem *The Devil's Tribute to Moling*[2] from the notes to the Calendar of Oengus; for example: "He is a blind nut in which there is no good, a stinking rottenness, a withered tree, a bough of the crab-apple without blossom, who does not do the will of the King".

On the whole, observation of nature took a rather different turn in the Western languages, and expressed itself as gnomic poetry, riddle poetry, and catechisms of physical lore. The first, nature gnomes, are of considerable importance in early Welsh poetry and in Anglo-Saxon, though not at all in Irish and Norse, and they will be dealt with in Chapter III. The second, riddles, are a large and remarkable group in Anglo-Saxon,[3] and many of them are little nature poems on animals, elements, and the rest; for example the riddle no. 30 in the Exeter Book:

I saw a creature in wondrous wise carrying booty between its horns, a bright heavenly vessel cunningly adorned, a booty homewards from the plunder raid; it would build itself a bower in its castle, to set it up skilfully if it might so be. Then came a wondrous creature over the hilltop, one that is well known to all dwellers on earth; it took away the booty and drove home the wanderer against its will; then it went westward thence, going in enmity, and hastened away. Dust rose to heaven, dew

[1] *Rhieingerddi y Gogynfeirdd* (Denbigh, 1915), pp. 27 ff.
[2] Ed. and tr. Stokes, *Félire Oengusso Céli Dé*, p. 156; tr. Anc. I. p. 39.
[3] See Tupper, *The Riddles of the Exeter Book* (Albion Series, 1910); and A. J. Wyatt, *Old English Riddles* (Belles-Lettres Series, Boston, 1912).

fell on earth, night passed away; and no man after knew where that creature went.[1]

The answer is the moon being driven away by the sun at sunrise. A case in early Welsh—apparently the only one—is Taliesin's riddle on the wind: "Figure who it is, created before the flood, a mighty creature without flesh, without bone, without veins, without blood, without head and without feet...."[2]

The physical catechism and catalogue of physical knowledge, in which one party asks the other questions about natural phenomena or someone declares his knowledge of these things, occur in Norse, Anglo-Saxon, Irish, and Welsh, though in the last three to a very limited extent.[3] The Taliesin poems contain short passages of the kind, where the poet asks questions without answers,[4] but from the point of view of nature poetry they are rudimentary. Anglo-Saxon has also another kind of classifying poetry, the alphabetic "Runic" poem, in which the names of the letters in the Runic alphabet are made the subject of descriptive verses as in the rhyme about "A was an Archer"; when the subject is a natural one, nature poetry enters in: "Ice is very cold, exceedingly slippery; it glitters glass-clear most like to jewels, a floor wrought by the frost, fair to look upon." "The newt is a water-fish, and yet it enjoys its food upon land; it has a fair dwelling encompassed with water where it lives in delight."[5] The type is not found in Welsh or Irish.

All these gnomes and riddles and problems and catalogues have not in themselves developed very far towards nature

[1] See Wyatt, *op. cit.* p. 22. [2] BT, p. 36.
[3] Cf. H. M. and N. K. Chadwick, *op. cit.* pp. 459–60 and 467.
[4] RBH, col. 1054.
[5] See B. Dickins, *Runic and Heroic Poems of the old Teutonic Peoples* (Cambridge, 1915), pp. 14 and 22.

poetry in the Celtic languages, but they illustrate very well the way in which primitive scientific nature poetry can come about, and this as we shall see may well be at the back of some real nature poetry.

Still another class can perhaps best be included here, that is, the List of Pleasant Things. The Pleasant Things of Taliesin[1] seems to be a kind of catalogue of these, and as it is a catalogue it is probably to be included in this group, for it has very much the gnomic spirit of observance and classification. Those lines of the poem connected with nature are given here; the rest deal with human matters such as banqueting, riding, religion:

> Pleasant are fruits in the season of autumn,
> also pleasant is wheat on the stalk;
> pleasant is the sun in the cloudless sky,...
> pleasant is the eagle on the shore of the sea when it is in flood,
> also pleasant are seagulls at play;...
> pleasant is May for the cuckoos and the nightingale,
> also pleasant when the weather is better.
> Pleasant is the moon shining on the world,...
> pleasant is summer and the calm long day;...
> pleasant are flowers at the top of fragrant bushes,...
> pleasant are the lonely doe and the hind;...
> pleasant is the vegetable-garden when the leek flourishes,
> also pleasant is the charlock[2] in the young plants;
> pleasant is the heath when it is heathery,
> also pleasant is the sea-marsh for cattle.

Poem XXII, Finn's Delights, is much later, but it is developed from much the same idea of description; the writer gives a catalogue of the sounds that were dear to Finn when he was alive, and, though a more literary composition and not gnomic in form, it is in reality as much a selection of Pleasant Things as Taliesin's. A still later

[1] BT, p. 8.   [2] See EWGP, p. 59.

Fenian poem on the same subject occurs in the Book of the Dean of Lismore:[1]

Sweet is the voice of a man in Tír an Óir, sweet is the strain that the birds sing, sweet is the crying the heron makes, sweet is the wave at Bun dá Threóir.

Sweet is the sound the wind makes, sweet is the voice of the cuckoo above Caise Con, lovely is the brightness the sun makes, sweet is the trilling of the blackbird from the west.

Sweet is the voice of the eagle of Assaroe above the pack of the great son of Moirne, sweet is the voice of the cuckoo on the bushy boughs, lovely is the silence the heron makes.

Fionn mac Cumhaill is my own father, there are seven eager battalions in his war-band; when he lets slip the hounds after the deer, sweet is their clamour on its track.

The last big group that concerns us, and often the most highly elaborated, is that which deals with places, where descriptive nature poetry is an essential element. A place can be treated as a setting, and that in various ways. It may be the scene of a story, when the nature element would be used merely as an indication of the immediate surroundings, for example the passage from Pindar: "But she hid him away among rushes and impenetrable thickets, his tender body drenched with the yellow and purple glow of violets".[2] Or it may be much elaborated, with sometimes partial attention to the plants and trees that grow there, as in the picture of Hylas' Well in the thirteenth idyll of Theocritus (ll. 40-5), and the other well in the twenty-second idyll, ll. 37-43:

And they found an ever-flowing spring under a smooth rock, filled with pure water, and the pebbles beneath appeared like crystal and silver in the depths; near at hand grew tall pines and

---

[1] A. Macbain and J. Kennedy, *Reliquiae Celticae* (Inverness, 1892-4), I, 82. See ed. in T. F. O'Rahilly, *Measgra Danta*, I, p. 87. Cf. also poem XXIII, and note, p. 41.

[2] *Olympians*, VI, 53-6.

white planes and high-crested cypresses, and sweet-smelling flowers—a toil dear to the hairy bees—those that blossom about the meadows at the passing of spring.

Here the spirit of description is very similar to that in poem XV. Or again the place may be an actual particular locality, which for various reasons comes to be described; perhaps there is a story about it which would involve its description, as sometimes in the Irish Dinnshenchas and the Agallamh na Senórach, and possibly in the quatrains nos. XXXVIII and XXXIX, whose context is lost; or it may be treated as full of associations for the poet, as so often in Fenian poetry, poems XV, XVI, XVII, XXI, XXIV and XLI, for example; or as a contrast to his present condition, a situation discussed in Chapter II. If the speaker has reason to describe his dwelling-place and his way of life there the scene may be described, as in the poetry of the Hermits (Chapter I). Little descriptive phrases may occur attached to place names, like $\pi o \lambda v \tau \rho \eta \rho \omega v \alpha \ \tau \epsilon \ \Theta \iota \sigma \beta \eta v$ (*Iliad*, II, 1. 502), "Thisbe haunt of doves", which is comparable to *Aran na n-aighedh n-imda*, "Arran of the many stags", in poem XVI. A place or district may be described in a poem where the speaker bids farewell to it, dwelling on his memories of it and on the various parts or aspects that he loved. Such is the famous "Deirdre's Farewell to Scotland" from the story of the Fate of the Sons of Uisneach (perhaps fourteenth century);[1] verses 4, 5, 6, 8 and 9:

Glen Lay, alas, Glen Lay; I used to sleep below the fair rock; fish and venison and badger's fat, that was my share in Glen Lay.

Glen Massan, alas, Glen Massan, tall was its garlic, bright its grasses; we used to have a light sleep above the wooded river-mouth of Glen Massan.

---

[1] Ed. and tr. R. J. O'Duffy, *Oidhe Cloinne Uisnigh* (Soc. for the Preservation of the Irish Lang., 1898), pp. 18–19.

Glen Etive, alas, Glen Etive, it was there I raised my first house; lovely was its wood when we arose, a dwelling of the sun was Glen Etive....

Glen Dá Ruadh, alas, Glen Dá Ruadh, greeting to every man who is its native; melodious is the voice of the cuckoo on the bending bough on the crest above Glen Dá Ruadh.

Beloved is Draighen above the firm beach, beloved is its water over the pure sand; I would not have come away from it if I had not come with my beloved.

So with another poem attributed to Deirdre (no. XLI) which belongs to the same sphere of ideas, and no doubt implies a farewell though none is expressed. Compare the Farewell ascribed to St Columba, probably of the twelfth century.[1] Verses 1, 6, 9, 22 and 24:

Delightful to be on the Hill of Howth before going across the white-haired sea; the dashing of the wave on its face, the bareness of its shores and its border.....

I stretch my vision across the brine to the plain of plenteous oak-trees; many are the tears of my clear grey slow eye as I look back upon Ireland....

Many in the west are the fruits of the apple-trees, many are the kings and princes, many are the sloes without stinting, many are the oakwoods of splendid mast....

Beloved are Durrow and Derry, beloved is pure Raphoe, beloved is Drumhome of fine mast, beloved are Swords and Kells....

Delightful it is and delightful, the purple seas where the gulls cry; on my coming from Derry afar it is calm and it is delightful.

It is well known how similar these poems are to the "Boasting" of Hywel ab Owein Gwynedd (see p. 194); but Hywel's poem is not a farewell and really belongs to a different class, in spite of the fact that he chose to describe a district, and that in terms very like the last verse of the

---

[1] See W. Reeves, *The Life of St Columba* (The Irish Archaeological and Celtic Society, Dublin 1857), p. 285; and KM, Anc. I. p. 85.

first Deirdre poem or the fourth quoted from St Columba's Farewell. It is probably nearest of all to poem XXII.

Sea poetry is not uncommon in some literatures, for example in Greek, where, though it is rare enough by itself, in conjunction with other motifs it is frequent.[1] Welsh literature in our period scarcely ever seems to feel any emotion for the sea. The early Welsh were not a seafaring people, and references to sailing are mostly confined to the purely necessitous side of it. The different attitude of Anglo-Saxon poetry, so full of the sea, is interesting in this connection; the early English felt it to be a sufficiently grey and cheerless element and yet took a grim pleasure in its moods. So in the Runic poem:[2] "The ocean is a tedious thing for men if they sail in a tossing bark and the sea-waves greatly alarm them and the sea-steed cares not for the bridle." Compare the passages quoted on p. 113. Certainly the most remarkable treatment of the sea is found in Irish, where it is regarded with a genuine delight mingled with terror; this can be illustrated from many Irish texts, but nowhere so finely as in poem XXXII, with its fierce exultation in the storm at sea, worthy of the Vikings for whom tradition says it was composed. The Irish were great and amazingly adventurous sailors, and a dictum of Mr Sikes', made of the Greeks, applies very well to their literature in contrast to the Welsh: "It needs, perhaps, a seafaring people to admire a rough sea, even in safety on the shore."[3] The little verse no. XXXV also expresses in a small compass the same delight, while XXXIII shows a joy of a rather different kind. The simile of the sea's "hair" is found again in no. XXXIV on the drowning of Conaing; it became a commonplace in later Irish poetry. Verse 24 of

[1] E.g. in some pieces in the Anthology; many passages in Homer, etc.
[2] B. Dickins, *op. cit.* p. 18.
[3] E. E. Sikes, *Roman Poetry* (Methuen, 1923), p. 127.

Columba's Farewell gives us the calm sea instead; and poem VI attributed to him has a good deal to say about the sea.

These then are some of the more outstanding ways in which man has come to interest himself in nature, whether through his religion or through everyday observances of weather, seasons, and natural phenomena; or whether in a more literary phase as material for comparisons, embellishments, and descriptions of settings.

CHAPTER I

HERMIT POETRY

The poems in this group are nos. I–X.[1] They are dated between about A.D. 800 and 1000, and are mostly stated or implied to be the work of monks or hermits.[2] No Welsh poems belong here.[3]

Ascetic anchoritism had been practised by individuals from the beginnings of Christianity, but it was not till the third century that it became an institution of very great importance to the Church. Mainly as a result of the Decian persecutions there arose in the Christian communities of Egypt at that time a feeling that any relations with the pagan and any compromise with the ordinary world were unsatisfactory. Small communities were formed in desert places, where the persecuted and dissatisfied could live freely their idea of the holy life—an uncompromising rejection of the world—in the belief that individual spiritual purity and communion with God were only to be attained by asceticism. It was essentially an individual and solitary creed, and its followers, when not actually solitaries, were yet isolated together with their few companions by contrast

---

[1] The poem VI has not been included with the others in this chapter except incidentally because it is considerably later than the rest and belongs to the group of poems all of about the same date which are ascribed to Columba (see p. 90), and which seem related stylistically to the Fenian poetry. It is perhaps a stray imitation of the hermit literature.

[2] Nos. VII–X show no evidence, internal or external, to prove that they are hermit poems; they have no context, and may be mere fragments. They are included here because they seem to have the same characteristics as the rest.

[3] See pp. 178 ff.

with the rest of mankind. These ideas we shall find appearing in the Irish hermit literature.

The new asceticism was suited to the temperament of the Christian world in the East, and the communities grew, became important monasteries, and founded new centres or sent out solitary anchorites. About A.D. 320 two monks, Pachomius and Palaemon, drew up a Monastic Rule to regulate the constitutions of existing monasteries, and to be a model for the foundation of fresh ones. In A.D. 400 the monastic system was introduced into the Western Mediterranean world when Honoratus, a monk brought up under the Pachomian rule, founded a monastery at Lérins; it became the parent of other great monasteries in Gaul, and through them monasticism spread to Britain and Ireland.

The arrival of the new movement in the West coincided more or less with a critical period in the history of the Celtic Church. In Britain during the early fifth century the episcopal organisation centred in the Roman provincial cities was being broken up owing to the fall of Roman rule and the loss of the ecclesiastical centres to the heathen English. St Germanus' two visits from Gaul, in 429 and 447, may have helped to introduce the new ideas; but in any case by the sixth century missionaries from Gaul and Brittany had turned the Welsh Church into one predominantly monastic.[1] Christianity was perhaps already beginning to penetrate into Ireland in the first third of the fifth century, probably strongly affected by the new Gaulish monasticism; Ciaran of Saighir, traditionally an elder contemporary of St Patrick, was a hermit, and Patrick himself came under the influence of Lérins, though his own organisation in Ireland seems to have been episcopal. From the next century onwards monasticism and anchoritism flourished exceedingly in Ireland and Wales. As in the case of the original movement in Egypt,

[1] Cf. J. E. Lloyd, *History of Wales* (London, 1911), vol. I, ch. 5, § 3.

the two aspects were not very distinct. The monastery was often simply a community of hermits, always ready to send out smaller branches or solitary anchorites; so in poem III the hermitage described is to house a band of thirteen, but the hermit of the poem on pp. 105 ff. stresses continually that he is to be "all alone". Sometimes hermits would be attached to monasteries, like the "holy man" who lived near Bangor and was consulted by the Welsh ecclesiastics before Augustine's second meeting with them.[1] There is nothing to show that these early ascetics were particularly and characteristically concerned with the making of poetry, and it is probable that but for one thing there would have been no Irish hermit poems at all.

That thing is the great Irish anchorite movement of the eighth to tenth centuries reconstructed by Dr Robin Flower.[2] Dr Flower has shown that there was a revival of ascetic monasticism and anchoritism in the eighth century under Maelruain, founder and abbot of Tallaght, and Duiblitir, abbot of Finglas. Fresh monastic foundations were its outcome, and various Rules for the ordering of monastic life were drawn up, such as the Penitential devised by a congress of anchorites and scribes under Duiblitir at Tara in A.D. 780. Most of the important ecclesiastical works of the period, the Stowe Missal, the Calendar of Oengus, the Martyrology of Tallaght, the various Penitentials, and possibly the Triads, were the product of this movement. It was "the most prominent fact in the church of Ireland in the late eighth and early ninth centuries", "already active in the first half of the eighth, but it appears to have produced its most

---

[1] Bede, *Hist. Eccl.* II, 2. Cf. the first article of "Columba's Rule" on p. 104.

[2] "Religion and Literature in Ireland in the Eighth and Ninth Centuries", *Report of the Church of Ireland Conference*, 1932 (Dublin, 1932), pp. 66 ff.

characteristic literary results towards the end of that century and the beginning of the next".[1] Taking the obits of the anchorites and scribes that occur in the Annals of Ulster in the period A.D. 700–950, Dr Flower shows that their relative frequency is roughly proportionate and that both are commonest in the ninth century, the inference being that scribe and anchorite, writer and ascetic, were often the same person and that the two were only aspects of the one movement. Now the poems at present under discussion date from the early ninth to the tenth century; they are expressions of the anchorite ideal or sketches of the anchorite life; one can scarcely avoid concluding that they too are the direct outcome of this anchorite revival, and indeed that they are actually the work of monks and hermits. Most of them are anonymous, and when the reputed author is named his date is a good deal earlier than that of the poems, mid-seventh century; but the reason may be that the actual author, in a society where personal literary reputation was of no account, wished to give his work greater authority by attributing it to some famous figure of the earlier Church. This may be the case with no. III, a ninth-century poem ascribed to Manchín the founder of the monastery of Lemanaghan in King's County, who died in A.D. 665; perhaps the writer was a monk of that monastery and hoped to glorify the poem by ascribing it to his founder. In any case it cannot be doubted that the poems were really written by monks and hermits, for their tone is far too sincere to be anything but the genuine expression of men who felt intimately and personally what they wrote about.

Two of them, nos. III and V, are a definite avowal of the hermit ideal, and the others bear more or less closely on the point. First, there is the little cell in the woods and wilds, hidden away from all but God. "I wish...for a secret hut

[1] Flower, *op. cit.* p. 70.

in the wilderness,...a beautiful wood close by around it on every side"; "I have a hut in the wood, none knows it but my Lord"; "The size of my hut, small yet not small"; "A little hidden lowly hut"; "My little hut in Tuaim Inbhir". The same love of woodland retreats is a constant feature in the Lives of the Saints. St Deglán "was in his beloved little cell which he had built himself between the hill and the sea in a narrow ground hidden away above the brink of the sea, and trees close it about in lovely wise; and it is called the little hermitage of Deglán".[1] Coemgen "designed in his heart to leave the world and the society of men, and to take a solitary hermit existence in the deserted ocean or on a very remote cliff where he should have no part ever in the course of human life".[2] Colman mac Duach set up a hermitage at Boirenn in Connacht; "he had an oratory in the woods and a refectory".[3] The scene of a monastic community in the forest is described in the story of Suibne Geilt;[4] "a lovely glen with a lovely green-gushing stream flowing precipitously down over the cliff, and a blessed spot there where there was a gathering of saints and very many righteous people, and many too were the fair and lovely trees there with heavy luxuriant fruits on that cliff; many also there were the sheltering ivy bushes and heavy-headed apple trees bending to earth with the weight of their fruit: and there were also on that cliff wild deer and hares and great heavy swine, and many too were the fat seals that used to sleep there on that cliff after coming out of the great sea beyond". The scribe again in poem II rejoices in the "forest thicket" and his writing under the green wood.

[1] C. Plummer, *Vit. Sanct. Hib.* II, p. 58 (Vit. Sanct. Declani, § 38).
[2] Plummer, *Lives of the Irish Saints*, I; Coemgen, III, ii, 4 ff.
[3] RC, XXVI, p. 372.
[4] *The Adventures of Suibhne Geilt*, ed. and tr. J. G. O'Keeffe, chap. 72.

Then there is an evident interest in the simple fare and ascetic way of life. It is part of the hermit's rule to eat and drink only what is to be found in the surrounding woods or what he can grow in his own garden; he must be self-supporting and the plainest berries and nuts must be sufficient.[1] Manchín wishes for "a choice plot with abundant bounties which would be good for every plant", where he would get "fragrant fresh leeks, hens, salmon, trout, bees". The poem no. V, "King and Hermit", is largely an enumeration of the rustic foods which are found so plentifully around Marbhán's cell: "An excellent spring, a cup of noble water to drink"; "Acorns, spare berries... a clutch of eggs, honey, produce of wild onions—God has sent it—sweet apples, red whortleberries, crowberries". The Latin version of the Life of St Brendan tells how Barrinthus and his friends came to an island hermit-monastery (*heremitiorum*) where they were greeted lovingly by the brethren who lived there in harmony in all things; "for no other food or drink was served there but the roots of herbs and the fruits of the trees, and drink of water to sate their thirst".[2] The Irish version of the same passage[3] tells that "they had no diet but apples and nuts and the roots of every kind of herb that they could find". The passage quoted above from the story of Colman mac Duach continues "The skins of the wild deer were the clothing that they had; watercress too and water and plants of the woods were what they used to live on at that time". Coemgen, when he had settled on his hermitage at Glendaloch after the resolution described above, lived "without food but nuts of the wood and plants of the ground and pure

[1] For regulations of monkish diet, see E. Gwynn, *The Rule of Tallaght* (Hermathena, no. XLIV, 2nd supplement) (Dublin, 1927), Teaching of Maelruain, §§ 1–3, 8–9, and The Rule of the Céli Dé, §§ 2–11.
[2] Plummer, *Vit. Sanct. Hib.* p. 105, lines 8 ff.
[3] Plummer, *Lives of the Irish Saints*, Brendan, § 30.

water to drink; and he had no bed but a pillow of stone under his head and a flag under him and a flag on each side of him, and he had no dwelling above him, and the skins of wild beasts were clothing for him". Other versions of his life mention nettles, sorrel, garlic, meadow-sorrel, and many other plants.[1] A verse preserved in the commentary to the Calendar of Oengus tells how "Tigernach sang:

> 'A scrap of fine barley bread,
> that was my portion on the board;
> a shoot of watercress and warm water,
> that was my portion every night'."[2]

In the notes to March 5th in the Leabhar Breacc copy[3] the same commentary says of Ciaran of Saighir: "And this was his meal every night, a little scrap of barley bread and two roots of *murathach* and spring water; the skins of wild fawns were his clothing, and a damp quilt upon them outside; a pillow of stone was what he would sleep upon always."

The ascetic fare, hard bed, and coarse clothing, were some of the means by which the hermits attained their chief objects, spiritual purity and communion with God unhampered by defilements of the flesh; continual prayer and penitence were to be their occupation, and peacefulness, free from disturbing emotions and alarms, was the way of life desired. Manchín would have "a clear pool for washing away sins"; the poet of no. IV says "I will sing my psalms... for the purging of my sins"; Columba, "It is for this I love Derry, for its smoothness, for its purity".[4] The hut in Tuaim Inbhir is "a place where spears are not feared"; Marbhán lives "without an hour of quarrel, without the noise of strife". Perhaps the quiet clarity of vision in these

---

[1] *Op. cit.* Life I, viii, 13; Life III, xx, 39.
[2] Ed. and tr. Stokes, *Félire Oengusso Céli Dé*, p. 110.
[3] *Ibid.* p. 88.
[4] Columba's Farewell (see p. 90), v. 19.

hermit poems was itself the product of the ascetic life, as such vision is said often to be.

One of the most remarkable features of these texts is their very intimate love and sympathy for wild life. The hermit delighted to listen to the "trilling of birds"; "The clear cuckoo sings to me", he says, "lovely discourse, in its grey cloak from the crest of the bushes." He comes out of his cell to listen to the lark singing away up in the cloud-dappled sky; he wishes "that I might hear the voice of the wondrous birds"; Manchín would have the surrounding woods "for the nurture of many-voiced birds". At Marbhán's hut "the she-bird in dress of blackbird colour sings a melodious strain from its gable", accompanied by "the songs of the bright redbreasted folk...the carol of the thrush, familiar cuckoos". One has been reminded several times already of the famous passage from the seventh idyll of Theocritus,[1] of the elms and poplars bending above, of the damson saplings bowed to the ground with the weight of their fruit, and now of the larks and linnets singing and the ring dove lamenting in the trees; but there is a notable difference of attitude which is one of the distinctive things about the Irish hermit literature. Theocritus only listened to the birds and noted that their song was pleasant, but the hermits did more than this; they lived so much among the wild creatures that they became almost one with them, almost own brother to them, as it were hardly conscious that there was any distinction of genus. We can see that the writer of poem V felt a vivid joy in the "peaceful company", the "grave host of the countryside" that gathered undisturbed about his house; his "swarms of bees, chafers, soft music of the world, a gentle humming", are more convincing than Theocritus' cicadas,[2]

---

[1] Lines 135–46.

[2] *Loc. cit.* lines 138–9, τοὶ δὲ ποτὶ σκιαραῖς ὀροδαμνίσιν αἰθαλίωνες τέττιγες λαλαγεῦντες ἔχον πόνον.

though ἔχον πόνον is a pleasing touch. The same sympathy is seen in the ninth-century poem of the monk and his pet cat White Pangur,[1] too well known to need quoting, where Pangur's "childish craft" of mousing is so delightfully sketched by his master and compared to his own attempts at solving problems of scholarship. It appears most remarkably of all, perhaps, in the following two passages from the Lives of the Saints. The first is from the Life of St Maedóc, of whom it tells us:

As he was walking on his way a she-wolf met him on the road there, and she piteous, exhausted, starving; she came gently and fawningly to him. Maedóc asked a youth who had met him on the road, whether he had anything he might give to the wolf; the youth said he had one loaf and a piece of fish. Maedóc took them from him and cast them to the wolf.[2]

The other is from the Life of Ciaran of Saighir:

When Saint Ciaran came thither he sat down there straightway under a tree, beneath whose shade there was a most ferocious boar. The boar, seeing a man, at first fled in terror, but afterwards, becoming calmed by God, it returned as a servant to the man of God; and that boar was the first pupil as it were a monk to St Ciaran in that place. For of its own accord the boar straightway energetically cut with its tusks saplings and straw for material to construct a cell; for there was no one with God's saint at that time, since he had gone off from his pupils alone to that desert place. Thereupon other animals came to St Ciaran from the lairs of the wilderness, namely a fox and a badger and a deer, and remained with him in the greatest docility, for they obeyed the orders of the holy man in everything like monks. One day the Fox, who was more cunning and more wily than the other animals, stole the shoes of his abbot, namely St Ciaran, and abandoning his chosen path, took them to his old den in the

[1] Ed. and tr. Thes. Pal. pp. 293–4; tr. Flower in T. F. O'Rahilly, *Danta Grádha*, pp. xvii ff.; tr. KM, Anc. I. p. 83.
[2] Plummer, *Lives* etc., Maedoc, II, xxxiv, 94.

wilderness, intending to devour them there. Learning this, the holy father Ciaran sent another monk or pupil, namely the Badger, to the wilderness after the Fox to bring back the brother to his place. And the Badger, who was well acquainted with the woods, obeying at once the word of his superior, set out and came straight to the cave of brother Fox; and when he found him about to devour the shoes of his master, he cut off his ears and tail and plucked out his hairs and compelled him to come with him to the monastery to do penance for his theft. And the Fox, compelled perforce, came along with the Badger to St Ciaran in his cell at nones, bringing the shoes unharmed. And the holy man said to the Fox, "Why have you done this sin, brother, which monks ought not to do? Behold, our water is pure and common to all, and the food likewise is apportioned to all in common; and if you had desired to eat flesh according to your instinct, almighty God would have made it for us from the bark of trees." Then the Fox, begging for forgiveness, did penance by fasting, and did not touch food until the holy man commanded it. Thereupon he remained in the fellowship of the others.[1]

A passage among the notes to the Calendar of Oengus for January 31st in the Leabhar Breacc shows well the same mutual feeling:

Moelanfaid;[2] that is, the abbot of Darinis.... It is this Moelanfaid who saw one day a little bird lamenting and wailing. "Ah God," said he, "what has befallen here? I swear", he said, "I will not touch food until it is revealed to me." Now while he was there, he saw an angel coming to him. "Good now, cleric," said the angel, "let this not trouble you any more. Molua mac Ocha has died, and it is for that that the living creatures are lamenting, for he killed no living creature ever, great or small, and not more do human beings lament him than do the other living creatures, and among them the little bird that you see."[3]

[1] Plummer, *Vit. Sanct. Hib.* p. 219, v and vi.

[2] Note that Moelanfaid was one of the twelve "folk of the unity of Tallaght" mentioned in the Book of Leinster and therefore one of the chief figures in the Maelruain movement; cf. Flower, *op. cit.* p. 70.

[3] Ed. and tr. Stokes, *Félire Oengusso Céli Dé*, p. 56.

The tale of Maedóc's alms to the starving wolf, an animal which in almost any other literature would have been hunted down without pity, and the charming and kindly account of Ciaran's "monks" and their backslidings, exactly illustrate the Irish hermit's feeling for the brotherhood of animals. This particular tendency almost to anthropomorphisation throws an interesting light on the psychology of the hermits. A desire for seclusion, abnormally developed in their case, was crossed by the instinctive need for society, and by making the animals their brothers they found themselves a substitute which was without the disturbing influences and temptations of mankind. And if the living creatures were their brothers, the more therefore were they all equally the children of God.

The solitary hermitage in the wilderness, the life of ascetic purity and humble piety, the spare diet of herbs and water, and the companionship of wild creatures, are the distinguishing marks of the Irish hermit-poetry. Manchín's final wish was "to be sitting for a time praying to God in every place", and it is this quiet feeling of humility and worship which gives the hermit literature its charm; a feeling well expressed of a monastic community in another country in the letter to Paul the Deacon[1] written not long before the song of Manchín was composed:

> *Est nam certa quies fessis venientibus illuc,*
> *hic olus hospitibus, piscis hic, panis abundans,*
> *pax pia, mens humilis, pulcra et concordia fratrum;*
> *laus, amor, et cultus Christi simul omnibus horis.*

These things were seen to be essentially characteristic of anchoritism, and the poems are natural expressions of the hermit's thoughts, of the emotional impulse aroused by Maelruain's anchorite revival; almost all except no. V date

---

[1] See Dümmler, *Poetae Latini Aevi Carolini* (1881), I, p. 69.

within a century of the Assembly at Tara in A.D. 780, when the impulse was at its height. The new spiritual exaltation brought about the same acute awareness of external things as the spiritual exaltation of love is apt to do, and the hermit looked on the world around him with a fresh wonder that forced him to literary expression. He was not a school-trained professional bard[1] and his sincerity would not allow him to write in the bardic manner, so that for all their technical competence the poems appeal more through their immediate sensuous vision than through their technique. Writing of this, Dr Flower remarks that in movements like Maelruain's "language ceases to be decorative and ceremonial and grows simpler and more intense",[2] and he instances the delightful marginalia of the scribes as examples of this spontaneous overflow of emotion expressed in the simplest and most vivid terms. The impulse, the matter, and the style are thus inherent in the Maelruain movement; but none the less the hermit poetry, and particularly its form, is a development through that movement from an earlier source, the Anchorite Rule which we saw went back to the Rule of Pachomius. The so-called Rule of St Columba,[3] which belongs to the period of the Maelruain movement, is an interesting example:

Be by yourself in a retired spot near a chief monastery, if your conscience is not prepared to be in the communion of the multitude....

Let there be a fast place about you, with one door.

A few religious men to converse with you about God and his testament, to visit you on holy days, to exhort you in the testaments of God and the stories of the Scriptures.

[1] Contrast the fragments by the abbot Colman mac Leneni (ZCP, XIX, pp. 193 ff.), who was.
[2] *Op. cit.* p. 72.
[3] Ed. K. Meyer, ZCP, III, pp. 28 ff.

Moreover, anyone who would talk long with you in idle words of the world, or who grumbles about what he is not able to remedy or prevent, but causes you the more distress if he is a tale-bearer between friends and enemies, he is not to be received by you, but give him your blessing straightway, if he deserves it....

Constant prayers for those who trouble you.

Fervour in singing prayers for the dead, as if every dead believer were a special friend of yours.

Hymns for the soul standing....

Three good occupations during the day, prayer, labour, and reading....

Follow charity above everything....

Do not sleep till you think it time....

Several points in this strongly suggest poem III, and it is evident that Manchín's song is as it were a highly poetical setting forth of an anchorite rule. A valuable link between the two, the prose rules and the full flower of hermit poetry, is provided by an Old Irish poem edited by Strachan (*Eriu*, I, p. 138) and Meyer (*ibid.* II, p. 55, with translation). It is a simple Rule for a solitary, versified; the poetic spiritual exaltation, lacking in the prose rules, is there, but it has not all the characteristics of developed hermit poems like Manchín's song. Several likenesses to Columba's Rule will be noted,[1] and most of the essentials of the hermit ideal—the hidden little hut, the renunciation of the world, the close communion with God, and the spiritual purity gained by fasting, penitence and prayer.

All alone in my little hut without a human being in my company, dear has been the pilgrimage before going to meet death.

A remote hidden hut for the forgiveness of my sins, a conscience upright and spotless before holy Heaven.

---

[1] Note, in Columba's Rule, *huathad cráidbech* etc.; in Manchín's poem, *uathad oclaoch* etc.

Making holy the body with good habits, treading it boldly down; feeble tearful eyes for forgiveness of my passions.

Passions weak and withered, renunciation of this world, clean live thoughts; this is my prayer to God.

Eager wailings to cloudy heaven, sincere and truly devout confession, fervent showers of tears.

A cold fearful bed, like the lying down of the doomed, a brief anxious sleep, cries frequent and early.

My food to suit my condition—the bondage has been dear—; my meal would not make me full-blooded, without doubt.

Dry bread measured out, well we bow the head; water of the fair-hued hillside, that is the draught I would drink.

A bitter meagre meal, diligently feeding the sick, suppression of quarrelling and visiting, a bright calm conscience.

It was a beloved token, pure holy blemishes, cheeks withered and sunken, skin shrivelled and thin.

Stepping along the paths of the gospel, singing psalms every hour; an end of talking and long stories; constant bending of the knees.

My Creator to frequent me, my Lord, my King, my spirit to seek him in the eternal kingdom where he is.

This is the end of vice among mansions, a lovely little place full of tombs and I alone there.

All alone in my little hut, all alone so, alone I came into the world, alone I shall go from it.

If of my own I have done wrong at all through the pride of this world, hear my wail for it all alone, O God!

It is evident that the hermit poets derived their form from the Anchorite Rules, and that the development was from those Rules through such poems as the one just quoted to the song of Manchín, and so to its final shape in poem V, *King and Hermit*.

Dr Flower has chosen a certain passage from the Táin Bó Fraoich to illustrate the clarity and economy which distinguishes the best in early Irish literature, and notes how "all the detail is clearly seen and precisely stated, the phrase does not go beyond the needs of the situation, but everything necessary is said, and from the simple expression the emotion of the moment disengages itself with the subtle overplus of poetry".[1] This is what is called style in poetry, a feature associated for most people with Greek literature; it is found in the hermit poems perhaps as much as in anything else in Irish and gives them, un-Greek though they are in many ways, an almost Attic tone. What strikes one most at their first reading is that they are simple, clear, economic, dignified, with the subtle overplus of poetry all the stronger for that. A similarity and a distinction between the Alexandrians and the Hermits has been noted already in the matter of bird songs; the same might be said about wider aspects of the two schools. Both consisted of men who fled to the open country from the complications that oppressed them in the ordinary way of life, "the world and the society of men"; that is the theme of *King and Hermit*, which contrasts the anchorite who has chosen the solitary life "without an hour of quarrel, without the noise of strife", with the king who has preferred the power and the responsibility and the perplexities of royalty among the ways of men, and now confesses

> I would give my glorious kingship
> with my share of the heritage of Colmán
> to forfeit it to the hour of my death,
> that I might be in your company, Marbhán.

It is seen in *The Ivy Bower* and in Coemgen's choice of a hermitage "where he should have no part ever in the course of human life". But there the resemblance ends. The Alexandrians and the poets of other similar literary fashions were men wearied with over-civilisation in a city environment, who ventured out into the countryside, admired its

[1] Byron Foundation Lecture for 1928 (University College, Nottingham), *Byron and Ossian*, p. 9.

charm and envied its inhabitants their apparently carefree existence, their *secura quies et nescia fallere vita*,[1] from a distance and with the eyes of a confirmed city-dweller. Horace has sketched the type,[2] the business man who pauses for a while to envy the existence *procul negotiis*, and the food of *herba lapathi prata amantis et gravi Malvae salubres corpori* which he had doubtless never tasted and would disgust him if he did; and then returns to his usuries and his ineradicable city interests. Such people did not ever experience intimately the rustic life they praise so much; and the result is the essential artificiality which always goes with this aspect of Alexandrianism, even in a poet so convincing and so unartificially artificial as Theocritus. The Return to Nature "has been interpreted...as a refuge from the city altogether, either to the country or to the wilderness. The Greeks stopped short of the wilderness".[3] The hermits did not; they were "Simple Lifers" who really did live the simple life, and that in its simplest form. They had known and felt what they described, they had eaten the sorrel envied of Alfius and knew how great the profit of mallow and asphodel.[4] The hermits sought spiritual purity in nature, but the Alexandrians looked only for emotional regeneration; the former was the more vital quest. Yet the ultimate significance of the hermit's relationship with nature is something that transcends both nature and hermit alike. The woodland birds might sing to him around his cell, but through it all, rarely expressed, always implicit, is the understanding that bird and hermit are joining together in an act of worship; to him the very existence of nature was a song of praise in which he himself took part by entering into

---

[1] *Georgics*, II, 467. [2] *Epodes*, II.
[3] E. E. Sikes, *Roman Poetry* (Methuen, 1923), p. 110.
[4] Νήπιοι, οὐδ' ἴσασιν...ὅσον ἐν μαλάχῃ τε καὶ ἀσφοδελῷ μέγ' ὄνειαρ, Hesiod, *Works and Days*, 40–1.

harmony with nature. This is best seen in poem VI, particularly verse 2:

> That I may see its heavy waves
> over the glittering ocean
> as they chant a melody to their Father
> on their eternal course.

It was from this harmony with nature, this all-perceiving contemplation of it, that the Irish hermits reached to a more perfect unison with God.

CHAPTER II

ELEGY AND FENIAN POETRY[1]

Poems XI–XXIV, and A and C; and see p. 123.

An elegy is not of itself a nature poem, but certain kinds of elegy can deal to some extent with nature. This happens when the poem is a lament spoken by some person in an out-door setting. The most common form is when the speaker is a wanderer or an exile or an old man or one out of his wits, who is contrasting his former comfort or wealth or power or happiness with his present miserable condition: "Ich bin einsam, meines Beschützers beraubt, Haus und Hof sind verödet, alle Freude hat mich verlassen, immer gedanke ich der vergangen glücklichen Zeiten."[2] If he happens to mention his immediate surroundings, whether lurking in the wilds or wandering on the sea, nature poetry will generally enter in; almost always the description is a lament. Or again, the speaker may mention that it is summer, and that the contrast of cheerful scenery with his own wretchedness makes it all the harder to bear; or that it is winter and he cannot enjoy its pleasures but only suffer the more for its hardships. Descriptions of the seasons or some aspect of them often occur here. Perhaps an old man will complain of the cold and compare his decline to the fall of the leaf; on the other hand he may speak only of his youth and the happy open-air life he led then; or one whose home has been destroyed and his friends all killed may describe the weeds

---

[1] The word "Fenian" is used here of poetry about the Fiana, to avoid the unfortunate associations of "Ossianic".

[2] Ernst Sieper, *Die Altenglische Elegie*, p. 13.

and briars that grow on the ruins and the beasts of prey that feed upon the dead.

The first group is very typical of Irish, Welsh and Anglo-Saxon poetry, though the nature element is generally small. Myrddin is the best known of this type, the Wild Man of the Woods. He was supposed to have gone mad in the battle of Arfderydd,[1] to have fled to the forest, and there to have lamented his past nobility and his present miseries and to have prophesied the future in obscure verses. He speaks as follows in the Welsh poems ascribed to him:

A sweet apple tree grows on the bank of the river; the steward does not succeed in getting at its fine fruit which I used to have at its foot when I was in my right mind, together with a fair wanton maid, a slender queen. For ten and forty years of outlawry I have been wandering with madness and lunatics, after blameless good things and the discourse of minstrels.[2]

O little pig, the mountain is green; my cloak is threadbare, it is not sufficient for me; my hair is grey, Gwendydd does not visit me.[3]

So with Suibhne Geilt,[4] the king of Dal Araide, who likewise went mad in a battle[5] and fled to the wilds (see poems XI–XIII). The ninth or tenth century Book of Acaill mentions him and "the stories and poems he left after him", indicating that there was a body of Suibhne literature in existence at that time now lost. He wavers between despair at his dismal surroundings and joy in their beauty. Thus in poem XI he complains

> Bramble, little humped one,
> you do not grant fair terms,
> you do not desist from tearing me
> till you are sated with blood,

---

[1] Traditional date A.D. 574.
[2] BBC, f. xxv b, 15,–xxvi, 2.
[3] Ibid. f. xxx, 1–3.
[4] Cf. IW in Bull. I, pp. 228 ff.
[5] Battle of Magh Rath, A.D. 637.

and how

> Aspen a-trembling,
> at times when I hear
> its leaves rustling
> I think it is the foray,

and

> The starry frost will come
> which will settle on every pool,
> I am weak and wandering
> before it on the peak;[1]

and in no. XII declares

> Gloomy is this life,
> to be without a soft bed,
> a cold frosty dwelling,
> harshness of snowy wind.

Yet most of no. XI is in praise of the trees and plants of Glen Bolcán where he is living:

> If I were to search alone
> the mountains of the dark earth
> I would rather have the room for a single hut
> in proud Glen Bolcán.
> Good is its clear blue water,
> good its clean stern wind,
> good its cress-green watercress,
> best its deep brooklime.

In these poems the nature element has been elaborated extremely, as contrasted for example with the passages in Myrddin's. The poems attributed to Queen Gormflaith are in a similar strain, contrasting her former royal state with the miserable condition in which she now is. She addresses her ragged cloak:[2]

> Many a patch upon thee, rag,
> thou canst not help being tattered,

---

[1] Verse 48 of the poem, Irish Texts Soc. XII, p. 41.
[2] Ed. and tr. O. J. Bergin, *Miscellany Presented to Kuno Meyer* (Halle, 1912), p. 352. Dated possibly twelfth or thirteenth century.

and explains the reason;

> Often I am in the clutch of the briars,
> and they twisting beneath my rags,
> no friend to me are the blackthorns
> and the bramble is an enemy to me.[1]

This is the theme of most of the Anglo-Saxon elegies, where the stock subject is the exile who is forced to wander over the sea or in foreign lands. So one of them tells:[2]

> How I have dwelt the winter in paths of exile, destitute and wretched, upon the ice-cold sea, deprived of my kinsmen, hung with icicles, while hail fell in showers. There I heard nothing but the harsh sea, the ice-cold waves; sometimes I had the swan's song for sport, the gannet's clamour, and the scream of the seabird instead of the laughter of men, the cry of the gull instead of mead-drinking. Storms beat on the cliffs, where the tern answered, icy feathered; full often the eagle screamed, with spray on its wings. No guardian friend was there to comfort my destitute spirit.

The same scene occurs in another elegy of exile:[3]

> Then again awakens the friendless man; he sees before him the grey waters, the sea-fowl that dip and spread their wings; frost and snow fall, mingled with hail.

---

[1] Compare Suibhne's verse on the bramble, and this from another Suibhne poem (Irish Texts. Soc. XII, p. 30): "Raw branches have wounded me, They have torn my hands; The briars have not left The making of a girdle on my feet". We may compare the detached stanza quoted in Cormac's *Glossary*, s.v. *aitten*, and attributed to the eighth-century poets Mac Samain or Mael Odran: "Let none hold dear the wood of Fuirmhe Where it grows about Tuirbhe; Its leaves wound me, Its thicket does not shelter me". Is this also a fragment of some early Irish poem on the same subject, the lament of the fugitive in his wild surroundings? Dr Flower remarks (in conversation) that Mac Samain was in fact supposed to be a Wild Man of the Woods. On Mael Odran, see pp. 122–3.

[2] Ed. and tr. N. Kershaw, *Anglo-Saxon and Norse Poems* (Cambridge, 1922), p. 21, ll. 14–26.

[3] *Op. cit.* p. 10, ll. 45–8.

A slightly different type, and nearer to the Irish and Welsh, is the poem called *The Wife's Complaint*,[1] in which a woman who has been separated from her husband is living in exile in a forest cave and lamenting her hard fate (ll. 37–8):

> Here must I sit through the summer day, here I must weep for my disasters.

(ll. 27–32)

> They made me go dwell in the woodland groves, under an oaktree in this earth-hollow; old is this earthen house, I am all broken-hearted; dark are the glens, the hills high-reared, bitter the ramparts, overgrown with briars, a joyless dwelling.

The motif of the briars will be noted. Other poems tend more to stress contrast, whether between the pleasant surroundings and the individual's grief or between his present wretched old age and his happy open-air life as a youth:

> When the wood puts on the fair colours of summer
> very ill am I to-day....
>
> In Aber Cuawg sing the cuckoos
> on the flowery branches;
> woe to the sick man who hears them perpetually.[2]

So in poem A someone describes the coming of spring and how it brings back to him the sorrow that he feels for his friends; and in the rest of the poem, how the thought of Christ pervades all wherever he goes with remorse for his wasted past.[3] There is a little English love poem of the

---

[1] *Op. cit.* pp. 32 ff.

[2] C, 2 and 6. This poem is an elegy of exile.

[3] The style closely resembles that of the elegiac poems attributed to Llywarch Hen, particularly C. Passages in the earlier part of A also suggest this; compare BBC, xv b, 8–10: *Guydi meirch ac imtuin glass uet a chyuet a chid im a g[u]raget*, with RBH, col. 1047, 19–20.

ELEGY AND FENIAN POETRY 119

mache for Hector[1] and of Mac Coisse for Maelsechlainn.[2] The great Welsh elegy on Cynddylan goes further than this; it speaks not only of the actual burial (stanza 17) and of the helplessness and desolation of the speaker, but also, as we have seen, touches on the eagle that eats the dead, and later on the other surviving members of the family and particularly on the speaker's own hapless plight: "Before my covering was made of the rough skin of the goat".[3]

The elegy where there is no lament for the dead but only for the speaker's self, may or may not be a final stage of development; to this belong the lament of the old Llywarch, RBH, col. 1036 (the *Wooden Staff* stanzas, etc.), and poem C, the elegy at Aber Cuawg; in Anglo-Saxon, the *Wanderer, Seafarer,* and *Wife's Complaint,* and in Irish the Suibhne poems and others. It is not a characteristic type in Greek. In any case, it is here that nature poetry really has its place, where the speaker is able to utilise it in one or other of the ways described above, though it seems to be inherent in the earlier stages of the dirge.

A usage of phrasing which suggests at least a close connection between the true keen and the personal complaint is the frequent "to-night" (much less often "to-day") of the elegies, indicating that the speaker is referring to the present. The phrase is *heno* in Welsh, *inocht* in Irish (and for "to-day", *hedió* and *indiu* respectively). It is found in one of the earliest known Welsh poems, three verses from the Juvencus MS.,[4] where it has the old form *henoeth*. So in poem C: "I do not deny, I am sick to-night" (but also, "Very ill am I to-day"); in the Urien elegy, *góae Reget o hedi*[6], "woe for Rheged to-day", and *y gelein veinwen a oloir heno*, "the

---

[1] *Iliad,* xxiv, 725-45.
[2] Ed. KM, ACL, iii, 305; tr. Anc. I. pp. 78 ff.
[3] RBH, 1047, 13.
[4] Ed. I. Williams, *Bull.* vi, pp. 101 ff.

slender white body is buried to-night"; in the Cynddylan elegy, *Stauell Gynddylan ys tywyll heno,* "the hall of Cynddylan is dark to-night", and *Eryr Eli a glywaf heno,* "it is the eagle of Eli I hear to-night"; the "Oianeu" poem attributed to Myrddin has *Bychan a wir Ryderch Hael heno y ar y wlet a portheis neithuir o anhunet,*[1] "little knows Rhydderch Hael to-night at his feast, the sleeplessness I suffered last night". In Irish, *ní te anocht,* "it is not warm to-night" (poem XVIII); *A Bheinn Bhoilbin as dubhach indiu,* "O Benn Boilbin that is sad to-day", and *Anocht is tearc mo charaid,* "to-night my friends are few" (poem XXI); Suibhne Geilt says "There was a time, though I be as I am to-night, when my strength was not feeble, over a land that was not bad";[2] and Gormflaith, "Sad it is, O Dun of the kings,...sad you are to-night after him".[3] This insistence on the time being night is curious, and further, it is sometimes contradictory. In the Urien elegy, besides the "body that is buried to-night", there is in the verse before the "body that is buried to-day", surely a more natural time for a funeral; and in poem C, "Clamorous are the birds, wet the shingle, the leaves fall" can hardly refer to night-time even though the verse ends "I am sick to-night". Hence we may suggest that in all these cases *heno* and *anocht* in elegies are stereotyped phrases meaning in practice simply "now" or "to-day"[4] and implying generally a contrast. This meaning seems not to appear in the dictionaries, but the evidence of the elegies

[1] BBC, xxviii, 6, 15,–xxix, 1.
[2] Irish Texts Soc. xii, p. 26.
[3] *Miscellany Presented to K. Meyer,* p. 346.
[4] Loth (RC, xxv, pp. 115–17) remarks that the Celtic day began with the preceding night, and that "night" in Irish generally means the night and the following day; so Deloche (RC, ix, p. 444), noting this fact, compares the frequent use in France in the seventeenth century of *anuict* for *aujourdhui,* and similar uses in the provinces at the present time.

shows that they could bear it.¹ Its use both in true keens and in the elegies of a more individual kind is another link between the two.

In some ways the life of the hermit and that of the exile or madman lurking in the wilds must have been alike; and though the essential characters of the two groups of poetry, defined in this and the preceding chapter, can easily be distinguished, sometimes the distinctions are blurred. Characteristics of the one group intrude into a poem belonging to the other because of the similarity of the scene. It will be seen (p. 125) that the elaborate insistence upon the wealth of woodland foods in *King and Hermit* does not properly belong to hermit poetry; nor does the dialogue setting, which, though it is utilised in that poem to bring out the contrast between the life of Marbhán and that of Guaire, reminds one that dialogues between madmen and those who come to visit them in their retreat (often to persuade them to return to the world and sometimes to ask for a prophecy) do belong to the theme of the Wild Man of the Woods. Myrddin and Suibhne are both visited by various people with whom they converse, and Mac Da Chearda has a dialogue with Cummene Fota.² Possibly the poet of no. V deliberately conflated the two types for his purposes. One need not stress, perhaps, the fact that Marbhán is supposed to have kept Guaire's pigs and to have had a pet pig³ just as Myrddin had, and that in the poem (verses 3–4, see Meyer's edition) he laments the death of his foster-brothers like an exile whose home has been destroyed and who has fled to

---

[1] Compare the ninth-century *Colman's Hymn* (Thes. Pal. II, 299), l. 3, *for a fhóessam dún innocht*, "May we be under his safeguard tonight"; the twelfth-century glossator explains the "night" as "the night of tribulation" (dark time), missing the point.

[2] Ed. and tr. E. J. Gwynn, *The Metrical Dinnsenchas* (Todd Lecture, Series VIII, RIA; Dublin, 1903), Part III, p. 200.

[3] See K. Meyer, *King and Hermit*, Introd.

the woods. In any case, the poem is later than most other hermit verse, and the religious element has been very largely subordinated to the natural setting which is itself elaborated for its own sake. No. XI shows a confusion found elsewhere in the Suibhne tale; the Wild Man should look upon his surroundings with despair and horror, as in no. XII, but here Suibhne rejoices in Glen Bolcán like any hermit, in particular in his hut, so typically a hermit trait—"Homesickness for my little dwelling has fallen upon my mind.... If I were to search alone the mountains of the dark earth I would rather have the room for a single hut in proud Glen Bolcán".[1] Lastly, there is a misunderstanding which seems to have taken place very early (see p. 35) about the hut at Tuaim Inbhir. This (no. I) is on the internal evidence clearly a hermit poem; the speaker mentions his "little hut" provided for him by God and Gobban, the legendary builder of churches and oratories,[2] where he is at peace from strife; and he uses the word *cridecán* of God.[3] All this is typical of the clerical literature and the Lives of the Saints. The poem lacks anything which can belong properly to the Wild Man theme or is characteristic of the Suibhne story; yet the scribe has written above it in the manuscript *Suibne Geilt*, evidently believing it to be one of the poems about him mentioned in the Book of Acaill. The notes for December 2nd to the Calendar of Oengus[4] say *Maelodrán .i. o Thuaim Indbir no Druim Indbir a n-iarthar Mide*, "Maelodrán; that is, of

---

[1] Cf. v. 18 of Columba's Farewell (p. 90): "were all Scotland mine from its midst to its border, I would rather have the site of a single house in the lovely ground of Derry". As this is a monkish poem, it is not out of place.

[2] E.g., for St Maedoc; Plummer, *Lives* etc. I, Life of Maedoc, 1, § 34; and E. O'Curry, *Manners and Customs of the Ancient Irish* (London, 1873), III, 34.

[3] Cf. other such diminutives in religious poetry; *Isucán* etc.

[4] Stokes, *Félire Oengusso Céli Dé*, p. 256.

Tuaim Inbhir or Druim Inbhir in West Meath". Now, the verse quoted on p. 113, note 1, as a possible fragment of a Wild Man poem, is attributed by Cormac either to Mac Samain, a known Wild Man, or to Maelodrán, who was thus probably a Wild Man also. One Odrán is mentioned in the Calendar of Oengus, notes to October 27th, "Odrán, a roving floating abbot"; and a note in the Leabhar Breacc adds, "that is, he went floating from Gair mic Moga, that is, an island in Corcaguiney. Odrán was a priest from Tig Aireran in Meath or from Leitir Odrain in Muskerry". The reference to "floating" may suggest the faculty of levitation supposed to be possessed by the Irish Wild Men. Possibly then the scribe of the poem knew of Tuaim Inbhir as the dwelling of a Wild Man and mistook him for Suibhne and so came to attribute a hermit poem to him.[1]

The poems classed as Fenian are nos. XV–XXIV. XV–XVIII are from the thirteenth-century Agallamh na Senórach; XIX is from the Boromha of the Book of Leinster (twelfth century), XX from the Metrical Tract,[2] XXIV is fourteenth-century or later. XXI–XXIII belong to the Modern Irish period, perhaps sixteenth-century, so that in date they can scarcely be called "early", but they belong

[1] It is worth considering that there may have been an Odrán or Maelodrán, hermit of Meath, one of the Maelruain hermits (the person who appears twice as noted in the Calendar, the great document of the Maelruain movement), and that he is the actual putative author of the poem.

[2] There is no context or statement with this verse to show that it is Fenian, and on the internal evidence it is difficult to assert definitely that it is, but the theme is similar to the Arran poem and the general treatment quite Fenian; Sliabh Cua seems to be a Fenian place, cf. poem XXII, v. 4, l. 2, "the sound of the stags about Sliabh Cua". No. XXII has been discussed elsewhere (p. 87), but it is essentially a Fenian poem.

to the tradition of the Agallamh and are a valuable indication of how that tradition survived in a conventionalised form.

The two most striking in style, two excellent specimens of late Middle Irish poetry, are certainly nos. XV and XVI. Their subject is the same, places which the Fiana used to visit, and the treatment, a sketch of their attractions, is similar. They have not the restraint of the Hermit poetry but instead an imagery delightfully vivid and unartificial, which contrasts well with the stylisation of the later poems and their uninspired lists of pleasures (in nos. XXII and XXIII), typical of the desiccation which came upon most nature poetry in the early Modern Irish period.

The Fenian poems are a great deal less elegiac than are the poems described in the first part of the chapter, for they are primarily records of the past of the Fiana; but the elegiac idea is implicit in most of them, the lamentation that all this is no more, and it is expressed in some. As a group they have certain characteristics which belong to the later Middle and early Modern Irish period, and distinguish them from the poems of the ninth and tenth centuries which as we have seen[1] were attributed to Finn. Most noticeable is the frequent occurrence of place-names, particularly those associated with the Fiana. It is perhaps due to that antiquarian interest in topography and legend characteristic of mediaeval Irish literature, as seen in the various Dinnsenchas compilations and in the Agallamh itself, where Caoilte describes the Fenian associations of a large number of places throughout Ireland. The poems in question versify these associations. The place-motif has a special form where animals and plants are assigned to certain particular localities. This appears once in *King and Hermit* and occasionally in the Seasonal poems, in no. XXX as many as five times; but in the Fenian group it is much extended and conventionalised, one place with

[1] See pp. 41, 43, 44 and 173.

its animal or plant closely following another. In the short poem no. XIX there are fifteen such phrases as "brooklime of Cantyre", and in XXII and XXIII it has become an annoying mannerism. Another peculiarity is the interest in woodland foods. It was shown that it is typical of the early hagiological literature and hermit poems to describe the holy man's frugal diet as one of his ascetic virtues, and perhaps later Irish poetry was influenced by this to develop a similar convention for itself. The treatment is different however, for in this case the foods are not catalogued to show the frugality of the Fiana but are treated with the joy of the woodsman in the varied and delicious eatables which he lives on in the wilds. This has had its reaction upon hermit poetry in the comparatively late *King and Hermit*, where the interest in food is expanded out of all proportion to such a poem and in a somewhat un-ascetic manner; and perhaps too upon the Wild Man theme in poem XIII, though there also a certain interest in foods, a complaint about their meagre nature, is natural. The variety of the plants and animals found in the countryside and eaten by the early Irish on the testimony of the poems is quite astonishing to a twentieth-century town-dweller, to whom "living on berries and nuts" seems such an improbable kind of existence. No. V mentions apples, yew-berries, rowan-berries, sloes, whortleberries, crowberries, strawberries, haws, hazel-nuts, mast, acorns, pignuts, watercress, herbs, wild marjoram, onions, leeks, eggs, honey, salmon, trout, water, milk and beer. No. XVI speaks of deer, swine, mast, hazel-nuts, blaeberries, blackberries, sloes, trout. No. XV has cress, brooklime, mast, trout, fish, wild swine, stags, fawns. In no. XIX are blaeberries, blackberries, apples, sloes, strawberries, acorns, nuts, pig fat, porpoise steak, birds, venison, badger fat, fawns, salmon, fish. No. XVII mentions blackberries, haws, hazel-nuts, bramble shoots, "smooth shoots", garlic, cress, *meadhbhán*, dilisk, birds, martens, woodcocks, otters, salmon, eels, fish. Suibhne Geilt gives his "nightly sustenance" as blaeberries, apples, berries, blackberries, raspberries, haws, cress, watercress, brooklime, saxifrage, seaweed, herbs, sorrel, wood-sorrel, garlic, wild onions and acorns. So Deirdre,[1] describing her joys during her life in Scotland, mentions fish and venison and badger's fat, significantly together and in the same order as in no. XIX, evidently a conventional grouping. The diet is then one of flesh of animals and birds, fruit, berries, nuts, herbs, shoots, and waterplants, eggs, honey and fish, an impressive and intriguing menu.

[1] R. J. O'Duffy, *Oidhe Chloinne Uisnigh* (Dublin, 1898), p. 18, verse 4, l. 3.

CHAPTER III

GNOMIC POETRY

Sententious verse may seem to us to have little in common with nature poetry, but the early Welsh poets thought otherwise. A "gnome" is a sententious statement about universals,[1] as well about the world of nature ("nature gnome") as about the affairs of men ("human gnome"), and the group of gnomic verses under discussion makes use of both. Poems H–K and the first eight verses of F are gnomic, that is, they consist almost entirely of unconnected gnomic statements, among which "The vegetable-garden is green"[2] or "The furze is sharp"[3] are as much in place as "It is usual for a foster-child to have luxuries".[4] But E and G and the last part of F are not exclusively gnomic, for in addition to the nature gnomes they contain descriptive statements about nature relating to particulars ("nature description"); "Mountain snow, white are the house-roofs"[5] and "(It is) Winter's Day, the stags are thin, the tops of the birches are yellow",[6] are descriptive statements about a particular scene. To make gnomes of the second quotation it would have to be recast "On (every) Winter's Day the stags are thin, the tops of the birches are yellow". The difference may not seem great, but actually as we shall see it is very important, and these two kinds of "nature poetry" must be carefully distinguished. I call the second group of poems,

---

[1] It need not be and usually is not a current popular saying with an implied moral as the proverb is, and it need contain no advice or exhortation like the precept. The "sentiments" of Joseph Surface were gnomes.

[2] I, 16, i.   [3] J, 14, i.   [4] F, 1, iv.
[5] E, 35, i.   [6] G, 3, i–ii.

those containing these nature descriptions as well as gnomes, "quasi-gnomic" to distinguish them from the pure "gnomic" poems. D has stanzas of both types; the eighth is a good example of a quasi-gnomic verse:

> Rain outside, it wets the fern,
> white is the shingle of the sea, foamy is the shore;
> understanding is a fair candle for man.

Here lines i and ii consist of four nature descriptions, and line iii is a human gnome.

The Welsh gnomic poems, however strange they may seem, are not at all unique; very similar sententious verse is found in other early literatures, particularly in Anglo-Saxon. There are two Anglo-Saxon gnomic poems,[1] one in the Exeter Book and one in the Cotton manuscript of the Anglo-Saxon Chronicle, both of the eighth or ninth centuries.

> *Scyld sceal cempan, sceaft reafere,*
> *sceal bryde beag, bec leornere,*
> *husl halgum men, hæþnum synne.*
>   Ex. Gn. ll. 130–2.

A shield is the mark of a warrior, a spear that of a freebooter, a ring is the mark of a bride, a book that of a student, sacrament that of a holy man, sin that of a heathen.

> *Forst sceal freosan, fyr wudu meltan,*
> *eorþe growan, is brycgian,*
> *wæter helm wegan, wundrum lucan*
> *eorþan ciþas, an inbindan*
> *forstes fetre felameahtig God.*
> *Winter sceal geweorpan, weder eft cuman,*
> *sumor swegle hat. Sund unstille.*
> *Deop deada wæg dyrne bið lengest.*
> *Holen sceal in æled, yrfe gedæled*
> *deades monnes. Dom biþ selast.*   Ibid. 72–81.

[1] Ed. B. Williams, *Gnomic Poetry in Anglo-Saxon*, pp. 118 ff. and 126 ff.

It is for frost to freeze, for fire to consume wood, for the earth to grow, for the ice to make a bridge and the water to bear a covering, wondrously to shut in the seeds of the earth; for Almighty God alone to unbind the fetters of the frost. Winter must pass, the warm season return, summer brilliantly hot. The sea is unquiet. The sombre path of the dead is longest secret. It is for holly to be in the fire; for the possessions of a dead man to be divided. Glory is best.

Clearly, this is very much the same kind of thing as the Welsh poems. Nature gnomes are even commoner than in Welsh; other examples are:

> Wind byð on lyfte swiftust,
> þunar byð þragum hludast. Cott. Gn. 3–4.

Wind is swiftest in the sky, thunder when it comes is loudest.

> Fisc sceal on wætere
> cynren cennan. Ibid. 27–8.

It is for a fish to beget its kind in the water.

> Fugel uppe sceal
> lacan on lyfte. Leax sceal on wæle
> mid sceote scriðan. Scur sceal on heofenum
> winde geblanden in þas woruld cuman. Ibid. 38–41.

A bird shall swoop in the sky above; a salmon shall glide and dart in a pool, a shower shall come into the world mingled with wind in the heavens.

All this reminds one very much of the Welsh "The cock's comb is red"[1] and "Usual is the nest of an eagle in the top of an oak".[2] So with the human gnomes. There are sentiments about kings and princes:

> Cyning sceal on healle
> beagas dælan. Ibid. 28–9.

A king must distribute rings in the hall.

> Cyning biþ anwealdes georn. Ex. Gn. 59.

A king is eager for power.

[1] I, 1, i.   [2] F, 7, i.

Ellen sceal on eorle.   Cott. Gn. 16.

Courage is characteristic of a knight.

Eorl sceal on eos boge.   Ex. Gn. 63.

It is for a knight to be on horseback.

So in Welsh: "It is usual for a prince to provide a feast";[1] "Bold is the chief and avid of heart";[2] "The knight is conspicuous".[3] Political and other institutions are mentioned:

þing sceal gehegan,
frod wið frodne, biþ hyra ferð gelic,
hi a sace semað.   Ibid. 18–20.

An assembly shall hold council, wise with wise; their minds are at one, they settle feuds ever.

Compare the Welsh "The word of a retinue is reliable".[4]

Pious sentiments occur:

God bið genge and wiþ God lenge.   Ibid. 121.

Good is enduring and acceptable to God.

So in Welsh, "Trust in God will not deceive you".[5] The exile is a characteristic figure in a state of society like those of early England and Wales. "The exile is an outcast"[6] and "Want befalls in exile"[7] are paralleled in Anglo-Saxon by

Earm biþ se þe sceal ana lifgan,
wineleas wunian hafaþ him wyrd geteod.
   Ibid. 173–4.

Wretched is he who must live alone, fate has decreed him to dwell friendless.

Women and children are a matter of interest at all times. "A bad woman causes frequent scandals"[8] and "Boys are nimble and grimy"[9] occur in Welsh; and in Anglo-Saxon

Widgongel wif word gespringeð, oft hy mon mid wommum biliðð.
   Ibid. 65.

A gadding woman gives rise to comment, often she is treated insultingly.

[1] F, 3, iii.   [2] J, 13, i.   [3] I, 6, i.
[4] H, 17, ii.   [5] F, 12, ii.   [6] I, 12, i.
[7] H, 8, iii.   [8] I, 16, iii.   [9] H, 20, iii.

> *Læran sceal mon geongne monnan,*
> *trymman and tyhtan þæt he teala cunne,*
> *oþ þæt hine mon atemedne hæbbe.* Ex. Gn. 45–7.

One shall instruct a youth, trim him and exhort him, that he may have good sense, till one has tamed him.

The sick and maimed appear in both languages: in Welsh, "The sick man is querulous",[1] "The blind man is a prisoner";[2] and in Anglo-Saxon

> *Seoc se biþ þe to seldan ieteþ.* Ibid. 112.

Sick is he who eats too seldom.

> *Blind sceal his eagna þolian.* Ibid. 39.

The blind man suffers in his eyes.

The Anglo-Saxon elegies employ gnomes sometimes to point a moral and sometimes in what seems a more irrelevant way. The gnome *stieran mon sceal strongum mode*, "a man should govern a strong temperament", l. 51 of the Exeter Gnomes, occurs as a general reflection in the elegy *The Seafarer*, l. 119. But the Anglo-Saxon gnomic poems show no trace of conflation with the elegies, as we shall see the Welsh do. The elegies of both languages have a common sententious outlook such as naturally finds expression in gnomes, in both sometimes with a certain disconnection of narrative which has led to their being taken for interpolations in the case of Anglo-Saxon or clumsy botching in the case of Welsh. If there were any Welsh heroic epic, no doubt the gnomes would be found there too, exactly as they are in the Anglo-Saxon epic *Beowulf*:

> *selre bið æghwæm*
> *þæt he his freond wrece þonne he fela murne.*
> ll. 1384–5.

It is better for one to avenge his friend than to mourn him overmuch.

In *Beowulf* the gnomes are concerned with heroic subjects and beliefs, as is natural in a heroic poem, and are mostly moralisations by the poet himself.

---
[1] I, 13, ii.   [2] H, 14, iii.

Gnomic poems occur likewise in early Norse;[1] but they show a high proportion of precepts, unlike the Welsh poems where precepts are almost totally absent, or the Anglo-Saxon where they are rare. Nature gnomes are uncommon, and are used mostly to illustrate some human gnome with which they are associated.[2] So verse 21 of the *Hávamál*, "Cattle know when they ought to go home and then they leave their pasture, but a foolish man never knows the measure of his own appetite." This is a very natural illustration of how nature gnomes could have arisen, but the extreme rarity of such cases in Welsh and Anglo-Saxon shows that it is not true for those languages at least. Examples in Welsh are D, 7, ii–iii, "A blackbird on its nest and a liar are never silent", and E, 32, ii–iii, "Water is shallow where it babbles, talking big increases the disgrace". In Anglo-Saxon the fall of the leaf is used as a gnomic simile for the downfall of the wicked in the poem "Solomon and Saturn":

> *Lytle hwile leaf beoð grene,*
> *ðonne hie eft fealwiað, feallað an eorðan,*
> *7 forweorniað, weorðað to duste;*
> *swa ðonne gefeallað ða ðe fyrena ær*
> *lange læstað....*[3]

For a little while the leaves are green, then afterwards they turn yellow and fall to earth and pass away and become dust; such then is the fall of those who for a long while commit evil deeds....

In spite of the differences, it is probable that the Norse and Anglo-Saxon gnomes go back to a common Germanic origin

---

[1] Cf. Chadwick, *Growth of Literature*, I, 382 ff.

[2] So with some of the gnomes in the Sanskrit Hitopadeça; e.g. "Glass by contact with gold gives forth an emerald lustre, so a fool by intercourse with the good attains to intelligence"; C. R. Lanman, *A Sanskrit Reader* (Harvard Univ. Press, 1927), p. 19.

[3] Grein-Wülcker, *Bibliothek*, III, 2, p. 73, ll. 312 ff.

and are therefore following a tradition of considerable antiquity.[1]

The Irish gnomic collections are chiefly in prose, and consist partly of "instructions" given to a pupil; the best examples are those contained in the story "The Sickbed of Cuchulain",[2] "The Instructions of Cormac mac Airt",[3] and "The Proverbs of Fithal",[4] and the earliest date in their present form from the early ninth century. Nature gnomes are very rare, but the following passage from the Instructions of Cormac is to be noted:[5] "*A huí Chuind, cid as dech do ráithib?*" "*Ní hansa: gem cain cuisnech, errach tirim gáethach, sam tur frossach, fogmar tromdrúchtach torthech.*" "Grandson of Conn, what are the best seasons?" "That is not difficult; a fine frosty winter, a dry windy spring, a droughty showery summer, a fruitful autumn with heavy dews."

This gnomic observation of the seasons is rather like a passage in the Anglo-Saxon gnomes:

Winter byð cealdost;
Lencten hrimigost, he byð lengest ceald;
Sumor sunwlitegost, swegel byð hatost;
Hærfest hreðeadegost, hæleðum bringeð
geres wæstmas þa þe him God sendeð.

Cott. Gn. 5–9.

Winter is coldest; spring most frosty, it is the longest cold; Summer is sunniest, the sky is hottest; autum is most glorious, it brings to men the fruits of the year that God sends them.[6]

The "Proverbs of Fithal" are on the whole nearer in their matter to the Welsh and Anglo-Saxon gnomes than are the

---

[1] Chadwick, *op. cit.* p. 386.
[2] Tr. Dottin, *L'Épopée Irlandaise*, pp. 123 ff.
[3] Ed. and tr. K. Meyer, Todd Lecture Series xv (Dublin, 1909).
[4] Ed. and tr. R. M. Smith, RC, XLV, pp. 1 ff.
[5] Compare the phrasing of the Ezra prophecies (see p. 172), with which there must be some connection.
[6] See pp. 129, 163, 191.

"Instructions". They are grouped together in lists, such as lists of "things that are better", "things that are beginnings", "things that are signs of something". So *ferr doairm díairm,* "badly armed is better than unarmed" (*op. cit.* p. 18); *ferr luaithe digairsi,* "speed is better than haste" (p. 26); compare in Welsh *g6ell corra6c no chebyd,* "the prodigal is better than the miser" (C, 4, iii). *Tossach dodchaid drochben,* "a bad wife is the beginning of misfortune" (p. 8), like the Welsh *g6ae 6r a gaffo drycwreic,* "woe to the man who gets a bad wife" (E, 17, iii). *Descaid serce sir-silliud,* "a sign of love is long looking" (p. 74); compare Welsh *gol6c vynut ar a gar,* "gentle is the look on whom one loves" (F, 7, iii). Such lists are found also in Anglo-Saxon, as for example this selection of "things that are most":

soð bið switolost, sinc byð deorost,
gold gumena gehwam, and gomol snoterost.

Cott. Gn. 10–11.

Truth is the most glorious thing, treasure the dearest, gold, to every man, and the old is the wisest.

In the dialogue of Solomon and Saturn:

Nieht bið wedera ðiestrost, ned bið wyrda heardost,
sorg bið swarost byrðen, slæp bið deaðe gelicost.[1]

Night is the darkest of times, necessity is the hardest of fates, sorrow is the heavest burden, sleep is most like death.

But such lists do not occur in Welsh except in such rudimentary cases as *Gorwyn blaen eithin a chyfrin a doeth,* "delightful is the top of the gorse and a secret shared with the wise" (H, 4, i). Much of the Irish "Instruction" literature was intended for the ears of kings and chiefs, since its avowed aim is the inculcation of the principles of just government; but the less specialised sections deal with much

---

[1] Grein-Wülcker, *Bibliothek,* III, 2, p. 73, ll. 310 ff.

the same subjects as the human gnomes of the other literatures, and often in not very dissimilar ways.

It appears then that gnomic literature of various kinds is not confined to Wales, but is found in other early European literatures. In the two Teutonic languages it is believed to be of very considerable antiquity (see p. 132), and though it might be rash to affirm that the Welsh and Irish gnomic literatures are similarly related from the beginning (for in spite of certain similarities the differences are even more remarkable), there can be no doubt that the practice dates from an early period in the history of both. The Welsh poems as they stand are comparatively late, but as we shall see some of the gnomes in them were already being used in the elegies in the ninth century; it is fair to conclude that Welsh gnomic poetry was in existence at that time, more or less contemporary with the Anglo-Saxon gnomes and the earliest gnomic collections in Irish.[1] We must abandon the theory that the Welsh gnomes are exercises in metrics strung together for the sake of practice with no attention to thought and meaning, or irrelevant and inconsequential maunderings, introduced without any sense of artistic unity into poems where they do not belong by versifiers so sententious that they could not resist the temptation and so incompetent that they could not complete their verses any other way. Some other explanation must be found. Leaving aside the preceptary gnomes, whose purpose is obvious, there remain human and nature statement gnomes. A probable explanation of these is that they are expressions of a desire for classification, for having the world with its chaotic variety formulated in an intelligible way; it is a step from the very

[1] Glyn Davies, *The Welsh Bard*, p. 89: "There was no professedly sententious poetry, or else the maxim would have appeared in its proper setting"; but the Welsh *gnomic* poems *are* professedly sententious poetry and the maxim *does* appear there "in its proper setting".

primitive state in which man feels himself overwhelmed by a mass of unrelated phenomena to one in which he is beginning to co-ordinate them and find his own place in relation to them. It is, in fact, the beginning of science, where the nature gnomes are the rudiments of physics and botany and zoology, and the human gnomes a crude psychology; and in this the nature gnomes, which seem so inexplicable to the modern mind, are just as much an essential part as the human gnomes.

The Welsh nature gnomes are statements about plants, animals and natural phenomena. The number of plants would be much smaller if it were not for the thirty odd *Gorwynion*, "delightful things", most of which are plants. The most frequent are "reeds" and "stalks"; the ash and the oak are common, and the birch, willow, apple, hazel, furze, heather, rushes and bushes occur more than once; while the lily, blackberries, bramble, earth-nuts, saplings, holly, elder, clover, wild rose, broom, iris, fern, charlock, rowan, hawthorn, cress and meadowsweet are also found. Of animals, the stag, the horse and the fish are frequent; not uncommon are cuckoos, deer, ravens, wolves, cattle, seagulls, ducks, hawks, blackbirds, hens, bees; and cocks, lapdogs, pigs, fawns, eagles and thrushes also occur. Notable exceptions are sheep, donkeys, rabbits and hares. The gnomes mention appearance, habits and habitats, such as that seagulls and lilies are white, that horses trot and wolves frequent the wilds, and that eagles nest in oaks and liverwort is found in rivers. The human gnomes—and these are by far the majority—deal with chiefs, religion, old men, married life, children, love, pride and oppression, cowardice, crime, folly and sin, the wicked and mischievous, and piety and ethics in general. Precepts, as noted above, are almost entirely absent, and the gnomes are not at all to be regarded as a handbook of moral instruction, though moral praise or blame is often stated or implied[1] without any exhortation to imitation or the reverse. Sometimes they show a very pleasing humanity and understanding of human nature; so H, 20, iii, "Boys are nimble and grimy"; *ibid.* 7, iii, "There is no modesty in hunger"; *ibid.* 11, i, "There is no formality in hardship"; F, 2, i, "It is usual for a portly person to be pompous". With so many observations on the world around, one should be able to form some idea of the *milieu* in which these poems were composed and of the kind of people who composed them, but they are of such a general nature that they do not give as much information as they might. It appears that the poets lived in a society where the king,[2] chief,[3] chieftain,[4] knight,[5] and the retinue of kings and princes,[6] were political and social factors; that is, perhaps, before the English conquest of 1282. They were familiar with the countryside and many kinds of animals and plants, and so must have lived an outdoor life, perhaps joining in hunting. They felt the contempt of the active man for the cloistered cleric,[7] of the warrior for the coward,[8] and of the leisured class for commerce,[9] but were not above hinting in bardic style that gifts are acceptable;[10] honesty and good faith and piety were valued by them;[11] they were familiar with the tavern;[12] they believed in good breeding;[13] and finally, they

---

[1] E.g. *gŏell hegarŏch no phryt*, "kindness is better than comeliness", G, 8, iii.

[2] F, 3, ii.   [3] I, 4, i.   [4] E, 8, ii.
[5] I, 6, i.   [6] H, 17, ii.

[7] F, 5, iii; presumably his own associates were reared in the traditional way on mead.

[8] E, 29, iii.   [9] F, 9, ii.   [10] I, 3, iii.
[11] F, 8, iii and H, 16, iii.   [12] F, 7, ii.
[13] H, 11, iii.

may possibly have been North Walians.[1] The type of person who seems to suit best is the bard at the hall of the country gentleman or small chieftain in the days of Welsh independence. The general outlook is too wide and perhaps not sufficiently aristocratic to be that of an official bard at a king's court, and though there is no reason why these should not have composed gnomic poetry the poems do not read at all like court-bard work. The Anglo-Saxon, Norse and Irish gnomes seem in no case to be the work of epic poets as such or intended for use in a Heroic *milieu*; we saw, for example, how the gnomes in the heroic poem *Beowulf* differ from those in the Anglo-Saxon gnomic poems. The virtues inculcated are not those admired in heroic poetry, not courage or generosity, but caution and other qualities conducive to worldly success; that is, the virtues of a later stage of society and perhaps a lower class. The Irish Instructions are addressed to princes, but only to advise justice and upright government, virtues such as would be appreciated by their subjects in general.[2] In short, it seems that these Anglo-Saxon, Irish and Norse gnomic collections are a kind of folk-philosophy adapted by poets in touch with folk-ideas and given a literary cast and setting; and the same is no doubt true of the Welsh.

It is commonly believed that the Welsh gnomic poems were composed by clergy, and much is made of their "moralising and reflective attitude". In objecting to this view one need not perhaps lay much stress on the unkind reference to clerical diet in F, 5, iii, but other considerations seem decisive. The tone of the poems is not at all what one would expect of a cleric, they are too much concerned with worldly matters and too little with religious ones; and a comparison with what is known to be the religious poetry

[1] F, 3, ii.
[2] Cf. Chadwick, *Growth of Literature*, I, p. 400.

of about the same period, that is, the religious poems in the Black Book of Carmarthen, shows that in fact when contemporary Welsh clerics did compose poetry it was in a very different strain. Why otherwise is there no reference in the gnomes to the Trinity and the praise of God and the Virgin and her Son, and the good of the soul, and the necessity of repentance to gain salvation, subjects with which the religious poems of the Black Book are so much occupied? Of all the human gnomes in the gnomic poems there are less than a dozen connected with God and religion, and those show nothing more than a vague piety. The nearest that the writer of religious verse ever came to the gnomic poems was in the Dialogues of Arthur and the Eagle[1] and of Llywelyn and Gwrnerth,[2] and it is obvious enough how different those are from gnomic poetry[3] and how much they approximate to poems like that on f. xlii b of the Black Book: "I enquired of the priests of the world and of its bishops and its judges, what is best for the soul."

In addition to the Welsh gnomic poems which are the subject of this chapter there is other early Welsh gnomic material in verse and prose of much importance for their origin and history, though it contains no nature gnomes. This includes the proverbial poem attributed to Meigant (BBC, f. iv), the poem *Gossymdeith Llefoet Wynebclawr* (RBH, 1055–6), the poem *Englynion y Clyweit* (c. A.D. 1200, ed. *Bull.* III, p. 4); and in prose, collections of proverbs and gnomes in the Black Book of Chirk (first quarter of the thirteenth century; ed. Ifor Williams, *Bull.* III, pp. 22 ff.), in Peniarth MS. 17 (c. A.D. 1250, ed. Henry Lewis, *Bull.* IV, pp. 1 ff.), in the White Book of Rhydderch (c. A.D. 1325, ed.

[1] Ed. I. Williams, *Bull.* II, pp. 269 ff.
[2] RBH, cols. 1026–7.
[3] In spite of the phrase "Eiry Mynydd" at the beginning of each stanza in Llywelyn and Gwrnerth.

Phillimore, *Cymmrodor*, VII, pp. 138 ff.), and the collection in the Red Book of Hergest attributed to Hen Gyrys o Ial (probably fourteenth century, printed from Dr Davies' transcript in MA, pp. 838 ff.). There is a translation and adaptation of the Latin *Catonis Disticha* in the Red Book of Talgarth written about 1400 (see *Bull.* II, p. 16), but besides being a translation, it consists of long preceptary sentences quite distinct from the gnomic material described.

Evidently there was going on in the thirteenth and fourteenth centuries a considerable activity in collecting, composing, and recording gnomes and proverbial sayings of all kinds, in something of the same antiquarian spirit as that which moved the editors of the Myvyrian Archaeology. At first sight it is natural to suppose that our gnomic poems are themselves entirely the product of this antiquarian movement, and since a number of their gnomes are found also in the prose collections,[1] to conclude that these collections or something like them were their source; in which case the poems would date from the thirteenth and fourteenth centuries. But the poems could not be simply or at least only versifications of the prose material because the differences are too great; there are no nature gnomes in the prose lists, while they form a considerable proportion of the poems, and preceptary gnomes are practically unknown in the poems though they are common enough in the lists. What did happen when the matter of the prose lists was versified is seen in the *Englynion y Clyweit*, where gnomes and proverbs like those in the lists are made up into englynion by taking any one gnome for the last line, ascribing it in the first line to whatever person would conveniently rhyme, and padding

---

[1] By "prose collections" is meant lists of gnomes not in verse form; the individual gnomes of those lists are often themselves in metre. The phrase throughout refers to the BBCh proverbs and the rest described above.

out the second line generally with some amplification or description of the speaker. For example, stanza 51:

> *A clyweisti a gant Gwrgi*
> *da y gyssul mywn cwnsli?*
> *"nyt reid y detwyd namyn y eni."*

Hast thou heard what Gwrgi sang, whose advice was good in council? "The fortunate needs but to be born."

In this case and in several others the proverb has been taken over in its normal prose form and forced clumsily into an englyn without regard to metre; indeed it is difficult to see how it could be put in englyn metre in one line. The first two lines of these englynion have therefore no essential connection with the third and are to be disregarded; and the whole poem will be treated for our purposes as a gnomic list like the prose lists, with their characteristic absence of nature gnomes, frequent prose form, and numerous precepts. But our gnomic poems are very different from this; the true gnomic verses are equally significant throughout, and the so-called "irrelevant" nature descriptions in the quasi-gnomic poems are not exactly parallel to the "padding" of the *Englynion y Clyweit*.

We have seen how the Anglo-Saxon elegies quoted from gnomic poems, and how the Welsh englyn elegies of the ninth century similarly used gnomes which are found in the Red Book gnomic verse. The Welsh gnomic poems cannot be dated so early as the ninth century in their present form, but it seems likely enough that there was a poetic tradition quite as old as that, by which nature gnomes and human gnomes were composed in verse form just like the Anglo-Saxon poems, and that this was the source for the elegies. The composers of our gnomic poems would then be making gnomic verses on a traditional model, using early poems, coining new gnomes, and even taking over current popular folk gnomes and proverbs. They were not antiquarians, but poets, writing as other poets had done before them. I suggest that they sometimes used folk proverbs, because passages occur in the poems which look like adaptations of popular jingles such as "a friend in need is a friend indeed".

For example,

Bei traethei daua6t a wypei geuda6t
ny bydei gymyda6c neb rei (E, 35)

seems to be a rather unsuccessful attempt to versify a saying which occurs in the BBCh list as *Bey dywetey tauawt a wypei keudawt ny bedey kymodauc neb rey* (no. 52). Such previously existing popular prose sayings and jingles may be the source of a few cases where the same gnome appears both in the poems and in the prose lists; but when a gnome like "The vegetable garden is green", obviously not a folk proverb but a gnome invented for the occasion of the poem, is found in the Hen Gyrys collection of the fourteenth century, it is hard to see how it can have come there unless it was actually copied out of the Red Book poem itself. The Hen Gyrys collection contains a large number of gnomes found in the poems, and some of them can only have been taken from the poems because they are misunderstandings of their phrasing; for example, the line H, 14, ii, *hir dyd; meryd mall*, "the day is long; the dullard is depraved", appears in the MA as *hirddydd merydd mall*, whatever the compiler may have thought that meant. The fact is, many old gnomes or lines from poems which were not gnomes were taken over into the late prose collections, either mistaken for proverbs or forced into some new meaning, and sometimes ludicrously mangled. So Engl. Clyw. st. 33, *racreitha dy eir kyn noe dodi*, "consider your word before declaring it", appears in the MA (Dr Davies' list) as *rhagnythed iar cyn dodwi*, "let a hen make a nest before laying an egg"; and an unedited series in Pen. 85, f. 19, ends *tuawc gwell korawc no chybydd* which is

GNOMIC POETRY

an ignorant, meaningless and mechanical transcription and misreading of the last part of C, 4,

> Coc lauar a gan gan dyd
> kyfreu eichya6c yn dolyd Cua6c;
> g6ell corra6c no chebyd.

So also even in the earlier collections; in Pen. 17 (no. 124) a line from B (v. 22, iii), *byrr dit; deruhid ych kighor*, "the day is short; your counsel shall be fulfilled", was mistaken for a gnome and rewritten as *byrr dyd ny deruid kyngor*, "in a short day counsel does not reach a conclusion". In the same collection a number of *bit* gnomes occur which are found in I and J, two of them coming together in the prose list (nos. 118 and 119), "*bit haha bydar*" and "*bit anwadal ehut*" which came together in that order in I, 10 also, *bit haha bydar, bit annwadal ehut*; a clear case of excerption by the Peniarth proverb list from the Red Book poem.[1]

If then our gnomic poems were used by the prose collections for material, they must have been in existence before that time, that is, before the thirteenth century. The internal evidence, linguistic and scribal, shows that the poems are probably to be dated in the early part of the twelfth century.[2] The date is confirmed by a passage in the Black Book of Carmarthen. On the bottom margin of f. xlii a couple of stanzas have been inserted evidently taken from some poem of exactly the same type as poem H, which itself shows that this type of poetry was current already in the twelfth century; and more, the second of them is quite clearly the

---

[1] But at this period the poems had not been written down in the Red Book, and if a gnome occurs in the prose lists in a form different from that in the Red Book, it is no objection to the theory. For example, Pen. 17 has *bit warancleu glew* where the Red Book has *bit granclef gle6*; but Pen. 17 was very probably copying from the Red Book's exemplar and the difference is due to the later history of the poem subsequent to the borrowing by Pen. 17 (see EWGP, p. 63).

[2] See EWGP, pp. 6–9.

same stanza as G, 6 and H, 31, with very slight differences (see EWGP, p. 8); the form of the stanza in the Black Book is most probably the original one.[1] The differences are instructive, for they are of the kind that comes about through oral transmission and variation and not by scribal error; the verse, belonging to a Gorwyn series, was taken into G by substituting the introductory phrase *kalan gaeaf* and clumsily wrestling with the seasonal contradictions which that involved. The same convenient shifting of introductory phrase is found in the later Eiry Mynydd poems in MA, pp. 358–62, where stanzas are taken over from the Red Book *kalan gaeaf* series for example into an Eiry Mynydd series by substituting the words *eiry mynydd* for *kalan gaeaf*; MA, p. 361 b,

> Eiry mynydd, caled grawn,
> dail ar gychwyn, llynwyn llawn,
> nag ymddiried i estrawn,

which is the same as G, 1, with *Eiry mynydd* for *kalan gaeaf*, and the third line (perhaps itself an accretion) omitted. So also the stanza H, 2, a Gorwyn verse, appears in C, 12 with a different introduction, "Fair is the upper part" instead of "Delightful is the top", and the third lines of the two verses vary in a way which can only have been caused by oral transmission; nor is it possible to say to which poem the verse really belongs, if to either. F, 10 is a stanza as clearly out of place there as it is in place in RBH, 1036, 29–30, and this, a case where a gnomic poem has borrowed a verse from an older elegy, seems due to same oral confusion. Such borrowings of whole verses are not frequent, but the

[1] BBC, xxx, 22, *kalan gaeaw gurim gordugor blaen gruc*, etc. is another case, which shows that Kalan Gaeaf verses like those of G were already being composed in the eleventh century; and it is significant that it seems itself to be an oral variation of B, 10 with the substitution of initial phrase described below.

Red Book gnomic poems commonly quote separate lines from each other in very much the same way as the introductory phrase is varied; that is, since there is little connection between the three lines of the gnomic englyn it is easy to forget the correct line in any given case and substitute for it some other one that rhymes. It has been shown elsewhere (EWGP, pp. 9–12) that the series I–J underwent very considerable oral variation.[1] Evidently then the Red Book verses were not simply composed straight off and written down at once in a fixed form on some definite occasion by some one person; they must have behind them a period in which they were being quoted and recited orally without any standard text, when it was easy for such confusions as those described above to take place. But the quotation in the Black Book shows that already by the end of the twelfth century they were beginning to be written down in something like their final form as it appears in the Red Book, so that this oral variation must have been going on before that time, perhaps for a long time. We have suggested that in fact the composing of gnomic verses and their oral and popular transmission goes back as a popular and almost folk custom probably to the ninth century and perhaps earlier; and that our gnomic poems, actually based on this, may even contain much genuine ancient material. But it is not suggested that the composition of these poems as they stand and their first writing down in a fixed form were earlier than the eleventh or twelfth centuries.

The later Eiry Mynydd poems in MA, 358–62, are interesting examples of the subsequent history of Welsh gnomic poetry, a monument to the persistence of literary

[1] Compare Glyn Davies, *The Welsh Bard*, etc., p. 84, but it is going too far to say as he does that in all cases where there is no end-link between stanzas there is confusion of order; the end-link rule is not satisfactorily demonstrated for these early types of englynion.

convention. They lack several characteristics of our gnomic poems and show many signs of degeneration, such as careless arrangement and mechanical composition; and a number of stanzas are only corrupt variants of the Red Book. Linguistically, they betray their later date; they have none of the early features seen in our poems, rare and obsolete forms and ἅπαξ λεγόμενα, "Irish" rhyme, and so on; and in a number of places they have forms later than the Red Book manuscript. For example, the poem MA, 360 b, beginning *Eira mynydd brith bryniau* rhymes in the first verse *bryniau*, *glynnau* and *borau*, which is not earlier than the fifteenth century. So the Peniarth 102 MS. of *Eiry mynydd gwyn tir pant* (MA, 359 a), rhymes *ni chwsg dedwydd hun foreu* in *-eu*. *Eiry mynydd gwyn bronn mur* (MA, 359) rhymes in the third verse *tre : angeu*, etc., with the same confusion of final *-e* and *-eu*. *Eiry mynydd gwyn tir pant* (MA, 359) rhymes *bro : garo :: eiddo : addo* and *Ionor : cefnfor*, and the poem MA, 358 a, rhymes *ros, agos, nos* with *achos*; *llog* with *chwannog* and *serchog*; *gormod, gorfod* with *dafod, parod*; all of which shows confusion of final *-aw(-)* and *-o(-)* never found in our gnomic poems, impossible before A.D. 1300, and very unlikely in rhyme before the fifteenth century. The opening formula was fixed as *Eiry Mynydd*, and as mentioned above, lines and verses which are found in the Red Book were adapted. The nature element still continued but was now very shrunken, a mere formula; the precepts were much more frequent, and there is a marked religious tone with a tendency in the long-stanza poems to end each verse with some remark about God. These last poems are written in a metre different from the englyn, a stanza of indeterminate length but usually of eight lines probably derived from English and French metres of the fourteenth and fifteenth centuries. It is used in the "Verses of the Months", poem K, whose general style and language are so similar that they must be of the same date and origin. It must be that the old gnomic tradition had lived on all this time, and new poems were still being written or made up out of the old. The poem *Gossymdeith Llefoet Wynebclawr* (RBH, 1055-6) seems to be in part an ancestor of the late *Eiry Mynydd* long-stanza poems; it has the same features of more frequent precept, rarity of nature-gnomes, and increased religious element, to distinguish it from the Red Book englynion. Perhaps the MA long-stanza *Eiry Mynydd* poems are a kind of conflation of this genre with that of the englynion, with that tendency to confuse what is proper to a genre which is a sign of lateness and devolution.

Prose gnome lists and versifications of gnomes continued to be made in England also well into the mediaeval period, about four centuries after the composition of the Anglo-Saxon gnomic poems.[1] *The Proverbs of Alfred*, an early thirteenth-century poem, consists of sentences of homily and advice, preceptary gnomes; and *The Proverbs of Hending*, written about 1300, is a poem in which each stanza leads up to and ends in a proverb. Hending was reputed to be the son of Marcolf, a character celebrated for his dealings in proverbial wisdom, just as some of the later Welsh gnomic poems were attributed to one Mab Claf son of the sententious poet Llywarch Hen.[2] Examples of Hending's gnomes are *Gredy is the godles* (i.e. the needy man is greedy), verse 15, and *frendles ys the dede*, verse 37.

The history of Welsh gnomic poetry is then something like this: from early times there was in Wales, as in certain other

[1] See W. W. Skeat, *Early English Proverbs* (Oxford, 1910), and *The Proverbs of Alfred* (Oxford, 1907); and K. Böddeker, *Altenglische Dichtungen des MS Harl.* 2253 (Berlin, 1878).
[2] See EWGP, p. 6.

countries, a habit of observing nature and man and a sententious turn of thought which expressed these observations in the form of gnomes, whether as rudimentary gnomic poems embodying folk-philosophy or in the tendency to gnomic utterance which appears in the elegies and elsewhere. Then, about the eleventh century, the floating poems which till now had passed about by word of mouth, confusing themselves with each other and interchanging stanzas and lines and initial phrases and absorbing prose proverbs sometimes in a clumsy manner, were recast and collected up by some one or more poets (probably lesser poets, attached to country gentlemen or small chiefs, the kind of poets who had composed and propagated gnomic poetry for centuries), partly rewritten, their language modernised, and much new gnomic material added; and were written down early in the twelfth century. Gnomic literature of various kinds must have been popular at this time; it appears in a different form in the dream-poem attributed to Meigant in the Black Book of Carmarthen, and some Black Book scribe was so impressed by it that he scribbled two verses in a blank space at the bottom of a page. In the next century and onwards antiquarians began to interest themselves in it and to make collections, both from the poems themselves and from other literary sources and from popular proverbs and sayings; such collections continued to be made or copied until the time of the last of the scribes in the eighteenth century and of William Owen Pughe and the Myvyrian Archaeology. Meanwhile the gnomic poems were still being composed and reshuffled down to the sixteenth century, generally, so far as is known, with the formula *Eiry Mynydd*; and "Verses of the Months", substantially of the same type, were widely popular in folk literature.[1]

[1] Cf. EWGP, pp. 14–15.

CHAPTER IV

SEASONAL POETRY

The poems are nos. XXV–XXXI; and A and B and the seasonal-descriptive parts of E, G, and D.[1] The Irish poems are all ninth or tenth century except XXXI, dated eleventh century by Kuno Meyer.

These poems are of three kinds; those that announce the arrival of a new season, those that describe a season in general, and those that are concerned with the weather.

The first group is, in Irish, nos. XXV–XXVIII, and in Welsh, A and G.[2] The Summer poems tell of May Day, that summer has come ("welcome, noble summer"), that blackbirds and cuckoos and larks are singing, that "the bitterness of bad weather subsides" and "rough winter has gone", "summer has come, winter has gone", that "blossom covers the world" and "green bursts out on every plant". XXVII and XXVIII on the other hand tell how "winter has come with scantiness", "the season of ice", and that "summer has gone", "low is the sun", "cold has seized the birds' wings". So the two Welsh poems; the passage from A starts with the announcement that it is May Day, just like the Irish poem XXV,[3] and describes how the birds are noisy, the woods green, the countryside many-coloured; and poem G proclaims Winter's Day, the Calends of Winter, with the

---

[1] See p. 127.
[2] The two verses C, 17 and 18, are likewise May Day announcements in series, exactly parallel to G.
[3] Cf. p. 178.

falling leaves, the flooded pond, the yellow trees, and the starving creatures. All these poems appear to be thought of as composed for the occasion of the day when the new season begins; that is the first of May and the first of November.[1]

This analysis reminds us of the famous "Natureingang" of mediaeval continental poetry. In the eleventh and twelfth centuries there arose in Western Europe schools of lyrical love poetry in Latin and the vernaculars; in Latin the school of the "Vagantes", the "Goliards", poor clerks and scholars who wrote and sang these songs for their companions and for wealthy churchmen who rewarded them suitably, and in the vernaculars the Provençal troubadours and the slightly later French lyric poets and German "Minnesingers". The fashion spread to most of the languages of Western Europe, including English, later Irish, and perhaps (as we shall see) twelfth to fourteenth century Welsh. One of the most persistent conventions in the new poetry was that by which a poem, usually a love song, was given a setting in spring, particularly on May Day, when the woods were growing green, the birds singing, the flowers opening, the day becoming longer and the air warmer—and, a common but not invariable corollary, depending on the nature of the main form—when girls and young men were rejoicing and it was right to love, dance and sing. Or it might be at the beginning of winter, when the trees were bare and snow and ice had covered everything, when the birds had become silent, the days were short and the air cold, and the time of love was over. These ideas are best expressed in the Goliardic poems; for example, from the twelfth to thirteenth century collection called the *Carmina Burana*,[2] as a spring-beginning to a love song:

[1] The beginning of the Celtic summer and winter. Cf. Loth, RC, xxv, pp. 125–30.

[2] Ed. A. J. Schmeller, *Carmina Burana* (Stuttgart, 1847).

SEASONAL POETRY

*Letabundus rediit
avium concentus,
ver iocundum prodiit,
gaudeat iuventus,
nova ferens gaudia;
modo vernant omnia,
Phebus serenatur,
redolens temperiem,
novo flore faciem
Flora renovatur.*[1]

And

*Ecce virent omnia,
prata, rus, et nemus,
mane garrit alaudula,...
pulchre canunt volucres,
nitet terrae facies
vario colore
et in partum solvitur
redolens odore.*[2]

For winter openings, which are much rarer than the spring "reverdie" beginnings, particularly in the vernaculars, note:

*Estas in exilium
iam peregrinatur,
leto nemus avium
cantu viduatur;
pallet viror frondium,
campus defloratur,
exaruit quod floruit,
quia felicem statum nemoris
vis frigoris
sinistra denudavit
et ethera silentio turbavit,
exilio dum aves relegavit.*[3]

[1] CB, no. 47.
[2] Ibid. no. 108.
[3] Ibid. no. 42.

In Provençal, a poem by Rambaut de Vaquieiras has the spring-beginning and the "Calends of May" continuing to the common theme of the Jealous Husband:

> *Chalenda Maia*
> *ni fueilhs de faia*
> *ni chanz d'auçell*
> *ni flors de glaia*
> *non es qem plaia*[1]....

The Calends of May nor the leaves of the beech nor the songs of birds nor the flowers of the iris do not please me so much....

Compare the dance-song "*a l'entrade del tens clar*"[2] which is a kind of operette about the Jealous Husband and the May Queen.

A very popular kind of poem with "Natureingang" was a conversation about love between the poet and some country girl whom he met in the country-side on a spring morning; the particular type where the girl is a shepherdess and the poet makes love to her is the famous "pastoral". An example in French is the following setting to a dialogue on the right kind of man to love:

> *Au renouviau dou tens que la florete*
> *nest par ces prez et indete et blanchete*
> *trouvai souz une ramée*
> *coillant la violette*
> *dame qui resembloit fée.*[3]

At the renewal of the season when the little flowers spring up purple and white among these meadows, I found under a bough plucking the violet a lady who was like a fairy.

As for the mediaeval German Minnesingers, part of a poem by Nithart goes as follows:

---

[1] Mahn, *Gedichte der Troubadours in Provenzalischer Sprache* (Berlin, 1856–73), no. 970.
[2] Appel, *Provenzalische Chrestomathie*, 4th ed., 1912, pp. 86 ff.
[3] Jeanroy, *Les Origines*, p. 466.

> *Ir fröut iuch, junge und alde;*
> *der Meie mit gewalde*
> *den winder hat verdrungen;*
> *die bluomen sint entsprungen,*
> *wie schône nahtegal*
> *ûf dem rîse in manger wise singet wünneclîchen schal.*[1]

Rejoice, young and old; May with its might has driven Winter away. The flowers have opened; how sweetly on the bough the nightingale sings a wondrous manifold strain!

On winter, an opening from the *Carmina Burana*:

> *Die vogele swigent gegen der zit,*
> *si lebent in grozen sorgen*
> *durh daz der vrost in chelte git*
> *des legent si verborgen.*[2]

The birds are silent at the season, they live in great sadness, for that the frost is ravenous with cold, through which they lie in hiding.

The new poetry appears in English towards the close of the thirteenth century; well-known examples are *Sumer is icumen in*,[3] apparently purely descriptive, and *Lenten ys come wiþ love to toune*.[4] It reached Ireland about the same time through French and English[5] and must have been adopted early into Irish, but this kind of poetry does not appear in manuscripts until the rise of the popular *amhrán* metres in the seventeenth century. The well-known song

---

[1] Bartsch, *Deutsche Liederdichter des 12.–14. Jahrhunderts* (Leipzig, 1864), no. XXV, ll. 83–8.

[2] CB, no. 142 a.

[3] *Oxford Book of English Verse*, p. 1.

[4] R. Morris and W. W. Skeat, *Specimens of Early English*, Part II (Oxford, 1894), p. 48.

[5] Cf. R. Flower in T. F. O'Rahilly, *Dánta Grádha*, 2nd ed. (Cork, 1926), pp. xv–xvi.

Fáinne Geal an Lae, a pastoral poem which belongs to that period, has a spring-beginning:

> *Maidean mhoch nuair ghabhas amach*
> *air theórain Locha Léin*
> *bhí an samhra 'teacht 's a' chraobh le n-ais*
> *is lónra te ó 'n ngréin;*
> *air thaistil dom trí bhailte puirt*
> *is trí bhánta mine réig*
> *cad a gheobhain le m' ais ach an chúilfhion deas*
> *le fáine geal an lae.*[1]

Early one morning as I went out on the banks of Killarney lake the summer and the leafy boughs were coming back with warm brightness from the sun; as I walked through towns and through soft level meadows, what should I find at my side but a sweet fair-haired maid at the bright dawning of the day.[2]

The likeness between this continental seasonal poetry and the early Celtic is very striking, even in detail. Both announce and describe a new season; compare *Chalenda Maia* with *Kalan Gaeaf*,[3] *Der Meie mit gewalde den winder hat verdrungen* with "Summer has come, winter has gone", *Iamdudum aestivalia pertransiere tempora*[4] with "Summer has gone", *Leto nemus avium cantu viduatur* with "subdued is the clamour of birds", and *Die vogele swigent gegen der zit, sie lebent in grozen sorgen* with "sorrowful are the birds of every meadow-plain".[5] The Irish and Welsh poems are not love songs, but the continental "Natureingang" is not prefixed only to poems on love. There is a whole genre, the Vision

---

[1] Version obtained orally from Peig Sayers, Blasket Island, Kerry.

[2] An English love dialogue where the spring element is reduced to a refrain, see K. Sisam, *Fourteenth Century Verse and Prose*, 2nd ed. (Oxford, 1922), p. 163: *Nou sprinkes þe sprai; al for loue icche am so seek þat slepen I ne mai*, "Now buds the bough; all for love I am so sick that I cannot sleep."

[3] And see p. 170. [4] CB, no. 95.

[5] Poem XXXI B, 4; see p. 162.

literature, where it is characteristic; the Vision of Piers Plowman, with its May Day morning on Malvern Hills, is a well-known example, and many others might be quoted.[1] The opening of the *Canterbury Tales* is a Natureingang to a poem that is neither a love song nor a Vision.

It is not possible that the Celtic seasonal poets could have learned this convention from the Continent, for the Irish type is fully developed by the ninth century, two or three centuries before the great continental vernacular movement and four or five centuries before it reached these islands. The two groups must be independent of each other, and the origin of the continental group should help to determine the origin and explanation of the Celtic.

The long-established theory about the continental poetry is that both the Latin and the vernacular schools derived from a supposed already existing vernacular love poetry among the folk, particularly in evidence at the rustic festivals which celebrated the coming of spring, and so characteristically including a spring Natureingang; and that when at the end of the eleventh century the cultured classes became interested in the matter of love and began to compose in the vernaculars, it was to these vernacular songs that they went for models. It is believed that there were at least two kinds of primitive seasonal ceremony; one was a sort of begging carol when a chorus went round from door to door announcing the arrival of the new season, whether it was a welcome to spring or a farewell to summer, and the other, with which it might be amalgamated, was a chorus of welcome to spring and the awakening of new life with dances and songs; and the whole was probably a folk survival of some primitive nature-worship. Spring festivities in honour

[1] E.g. the mediaeval Latin Apocalypse Goliae Episcopi (ed. T. Wright, *The Latin Poems of Walter Mapes*, Camden Soc. (London, 1841), pp. 1 ff.), and the Metamorphosis Goliae Episcopi (*ibid.* pp. 21 ff.).

of the new season are in fact well known to anthropologists in the folk custom of many parts of Europe, probably going back to remote times.[1] In England as elsewhere they were in use in the mediaeval period; in 1244 Bishop Grosseteste of Lincoln complains *faciunt etiam, ut audivimus, clerici... ludos quos vocant Inductionem Maii sive Autumni*,[2] "Moreover the clergy perform, as we have heard, mummings called the Bringing In of May and Autumn." As for the content of the early popular dance-songs from which the literary schools were supposed to have borrowed, it is assumed on the evidence of the literary poems and of such later folk-songs as are preserved that they probably began with the announcement that spring had come, no doubt amplified with rudimentary descriptions of the signs—woods green, flowers opening, birds singing, winter gone, and so on—and passed on to stress that this is the time of love when maidens rejoice and it is right to dance and sing. These various ideas had perhaps become stereotyped during the folk stage in certain recognised formulae in verse form;[3] but they must

---

[1] The French Fête de Mai ceremony, see Jeanroy, *Origines*, pp. 88 and 389. The same festival in thirteenth-century France in the *Roman de Flamenca*, where girls sing songs called *Kalendas Mayas*, "May Day Songs". In the fifteenth century, see Gaston Paris, *Chansons Françaises du XV Siècle* (Paris, 1875), p. 113. The *Pervigilium Veneris* seems to be a third or fourth century literary adaptation of some such ritual song, even to the extent of the choral refrain. It was sung on the *eve* of the spring festival of the Trinoctium of Venus, originally a popular festival. The homilies attributed to St Eloi (see D'Achery, *Spicilegium*, v), of which the latest parts are Carolingian, show that "walzings and dancings" and "choral songs" and "devilish (i.e. pagan) chants" were in use at seasonal festivals (primarily the Midsummer festival) very early. For other such celebrations in modern Europe, cf. J. G. Frazer, *The Golden Bough*, II, pp. 91 ff. Cf. the Rhodian Swallow Song.

[2] H. R. Luard, *Roberti Grosseteste...Epistolae* (Rerum Britannicarum Medii Aevi Scriptores, 1861), Ep. cvii, p. 317.

[3] Cf. R. Meyer, "Alte Deutsche Volksliedchen", in *Zeitschr. f. d. Alterthum*, no. 29 (1885), pp. 121 ff.

have been exceedingly rudimentary, for highly developed interest in nature and elaborate descriptions of it are found only in artistic poetry, never in folk-song.

Such has been the classic theory about the origin of the Natureingang. In recent years views about folk poetry have been considerably modified,[1] and some now believe that there is no such thing as a genuine folk poetry except in the case of songs which belong to the communal activities of the people, the *Gemeinschaftslied*, such as occupational songs and communal dance-songs. The history of the early mediaeval Latin love lyric has been examined by Brinkmann,[2] who shows that some of the characteristics of the Goliard love poetry can be explained from within the learned Latin sphere as developments out of a certain early eleventh-century kind of love poetry composed by clerics, out of hymns and ecclesiastical poetry, and out of Ovid. He tries to find the origin of the Natureingang in church ritual, but his arguments are far from convincing;[3] certain marked characteristics of the Goliardic and vernacular poems (notably in Provençal and the Minnesang) he has to admit were taken over from the folk. The existence of communal folk dance-songs on the Continent, a primitive *Gemeinschaftslied*, is in fact accepted by all,[4] and the most natural explanation of the Natureingang is still that it arose from dance-songs (there is good evidence

---

[1] Cf. J. Meier, *Kunstlied und Volkslied in Deutschland* (Halle, 1906), and Naumann, *Primitive Gemeinschaftskultur* (Jena, 1921).

[2] H. Brinkmann, *Geschichte der Lateinischen Liebesdichtung im Mittelalter* (Halle, 1925).

[3] It is impossible to deal with them in the compass of this book.

[4] Cf. Naumann, *op. cit.* p. 6: "Wir nehmen vor dem Minnesang heute kein Volkslied mehr an, wohl aber ein primitives Gemeinschaftslied." In spite of Meier and Naumann there are things in very early mediaeval Latin poetry and in the later literary schools which seem to suggest an origin in primitive folk-song even although not communal. One would like to see a satisfactory explanation of the *Alba*, which the derivation

that they *were* held particularly at the May festival,[1] in spite of Brinkmann), and that the later mediaeval and modern May celebrations were derived from them.

There is another kind of popular seasonal observance in continental folk custom, the Contest of Summer and Winter. In this two men suitably dressed take the parts of the two seasons and argue about their relative merits, and in the end Winter is defeated.[2] Alcuin's *Conflictus Veris et Hiemis* was probably modelled on this;[3] it is a series of amoebean stanzas sung by shepherds in the rôle of Spring and Winter, Spring praising the advent of the Cuckoo and the good things that it brings, and Winter describing his own benefits in reply.[4] The poem owes a good deal to Classical Latin influences, but certain touches, such as the fact that the two shepherds sing dressed in character as Spring and Winter,[5] are best explained as above. Certain contrasted Spring and

---

from the dawn hymn is not. The well-known tenth-century Latin Alba (ed. and tr. H. Waddell, *Mediaeval Latin Lyrics*, pp. 138–9; cf. W. P. Ker, *The Dark Ages*, p. 214), with its vernacular refrain, certainly suggests that some learned poet was adopting a folk convention together with its refrain in the folk tongue, and that *already in the tenth century*. Cf. Jeanroy, *Origines*, p. 75, note 1. Similarly with other themes in ninth and tenth century Latin poetry which do not seem to belong to Latin; cf. F. S. Allen and H. M. Jones, *The Romanesque Lyric* (Univ. North Carolina, 1928), p. 224.

[1] The twelfth-century Provençal ballad of the April Queen, *a l'entrade del tens clar* (see p. 152, note (2)), is allowed by all to be a slightly stylised festival dance-song, and it is absurd to say that its spring-beginning alone was adopted from church ritual when all the rest is a typical *Gemeinschaftslied*.

[2] See J. G. Frazer, *The Golden Bough*, II, pp. 99 ff.

[3] Cf. E. K. Chambers, *The Mediaeval Stage* (Oxford, 1903), I, p. 187.

[4] Cf. the verses quoted by Frazer, *loc. cit.*

[5] Cf. Frazer, *loc. cit.* In the mid-Rheinland Summer dressed in ivy defeats Winter dressed in moss. Cf. H. Jantzen, *Geschichte des Deutschen Streitgedichtes im Mittelalter*, p. 6: "der Geist (of Alcuin's poem) ist durchaus echt germanisch und volksmässig".

Winter poems in Irish may have some connection with a similar ritual contest (see p. 162).¹

The conclusion, if tentative, is that dating back perhaps to pagan times in Western Europe there was a custom among the folk of various kinds of seasonal celebration with songs sung by a chorus and chorus leader announcing and rejoicing in the coming of spring and the passing of winter and the reawakening of the world to love; perhaps telling conversely that winter had come and that love and summer were past; and an amoebean song between two leaders acting the parts of Summer and Winter in opposition. In the eleventh and twelfth centuries these were made models for some (but only some) of the themes in which the new mediaeval Latin and vernacular schools were interested.

It remains to see if it is possible that the Irish and Welsh seasonal-songs can themselves be traced to some seasonal celebration analogous to the Spring and Winter festivals of the Continent; not that these poems are themselves seasonal carols, but that they may be literary adaptations of them. The likenesses noted on p. 154 between the two groups of literature may be partly coincidences; but the general treatment, the season-song with full description, thought of as made for the first day of the season which is remarkably

¹ For later mediaeval conflicts of the seasons, cf. the fourteenth-century Low Rhenish *Van den Zomer und van den Winder* (and cf. Uhland, *Abhandl. z. d. Volksliedern Ges. Schrift.* III, pp. 17 ff.); for a modern Irish poem deriving from these continental conflicts, see Henry Morris, *Céad de Cheoltaibh Uladh*, no. 1. E. K. Chambers, referring (*Arthur of Britain*, London, 1927, p. 74) to the battle of Gwynn and Gwythyr every May Day in *Kulhwch and Olwen*, says: "Obviously there is a reminiscence here of the seasonal contests familiar in folk-custom." If this is true, it is useful evidence for such contests in early Wales; but it is by no means so obvious to the writer.

described as the *calend* in both,[1] is perhaps not a coincidence.

The two great yearly festivals of the Celtic world were on the first of May and the first of November at the beginning of the Celtic summer and winter[2]—*Céttamain* and *Samain*, *Kalan Mei* or *Kyntefin* and *Kalan Gaeaf*. If there were songs in honour of the new season it would certainly be at these festivals that they would be sung. The presumptive evidence from the poems seems then to be strong, but there is little support to be had from what is known of the actual festivals.

The ceremonies at May Day as described in Cormac's *Glossary*[3] and other early sources belong to a well-known pastoral ritual for ensuring fertility, but there is no suggestion of nature songs and May Day dances. Indeed it is very doubtful whether dancing was known at all in Ireland before the Middle Ages; there are apparently no references to it in the early native literature,[4] though there is a little fourteenth-century Anglo-Irish poem called *The Irish Dancer* in which the dancing seems to be regarded as characteristically Irish.[5] The same seems to be true of Wales, and the terms for dancing in both languages are late and foreign.[6] However, dancing is not essential to the hypothesis; season

[1] *Kalan Gaeaf* in Welsh: *Kalendas Mayas* in French, *Chalenda Maia* in Provençal.

[2] Cf. J. Loth, RC, xxv, pp. 125–30.

[3] See s.v. *beltain*. Cf. the ritual in verse 1 of the poem on p. 169, note (1).

[4] Cf. R. Atkinson, *The Passions and Homilies* (Todd Lecture Series, II, Dublin, 1887), p. 66, *clesaigecht 7 lemenda*, "juggling and leaping"; since it refers to Salome *lemenda* evidently means dancing, but it may be no more than a rendering of the Latin *saltatio*.

[5] Ed. K. Sisam, *Fourteenth Century Verse and Prose* (2nd ed., Oxford, 1922), p. 166.

[6] But they may have superseded earlier native ones; for Welsh Professor Williams compares *llemenig* in the prophecy about Gruffydd ab Cynan; see A. Jones, *The History of Gruffydd ap Cynan* (Manchester, 1910), p. 110. Cf. also note (4) above.

songs may well have been sung by individuals, or by choruses (perhaps female choruses as on the Continent) without dances. The tenth-century Irish poem called *The Old Woman of Beare*[1] has the words *it fáilte na hingena o thic doilb co Beltene*, "joyous are the maidens when May Day comes to them", and though this may mean nothing more than that the girls are glad at the coming of summer, when we compare the maiden choruses which sang the May Day songs at the continental festivals it seems just possible that it may refer to a similar celebration in tenth-century Ireland. Otherwise there seems no reason for the specific mention of May Day. The famous story in the Dinnshenchas[2] about the Samhain fertility ceremonies and the adoration of Cromm Cruach at Magh Slecht, if it is reliable, gives an indication of an occasion suitable for Irish seasonal laments at the passing of summer, though there is no evidence in the tale that such existed. Another and more significant notice is perhaps to be connected with this. There is a passage at the beginning of *The Sickbed of Cuchulainn*;[3]

A fair was held every year by the Ulstermen on the three days before Samhain and the three days after the day of Samhain itself, and the place where the Ulstermen were then was in Magh Muirthemhne, holding the fair of Samhain every year. And there was nothing in the world they did in that place but games and races and enjoyment and pleasure and eating and feasting; *and from this are the laments of Samhain throughout Ireland.*

The "laments of Samhain" are evidently a gloss put in by the scribe, and refer to an institution known throughout Ireland supposed by him to be derived from the Ulster

[1] Ed. and tr. K. Meyer, *Otia Merseiana*, I; see *ibid.* p. 124.
[2] Ed. and tr. Stokes, RC, XVI, pp. 35 ff.; see his references, p. 36.
[3] Ed. R. I. Best and O. Bergin, *Lebor na hUidre* (Dublin, 1929), p. 104.

Samhain festival; and it seems quite likely that these laments were songs bewailing the passing of summer, which ended according to Celtic custom on Samhain eve. Modern Celtic folk custom gives no conclusive support to the theory. In Ireland there are the usual Maypole dances and Samhain-eve begging processions, but no sign of nature carols with them. There is however a custom called the Bringing In of Summer,[1] by which at dawn on May Day boughs of various trees are picked in the woods and brought indoors to a song with the refrain "We have brought the Summer with us". Begging carols are sung in Wales by boys and girls on Calan Gaeaf night, and *carolau haf*, "summer carols", were sung in the Vale of Clwyd in living memory.[2] *Dawnsio haf*, "summer dances", are mentioned in 1823,[3] no doubt of the same character as the *carolau haf*.

The four Irish poems, nos. XXXI A–D, look very like an exercise upon the four seasons, not announcements of their coming but general descriptions of their character, evidently the work of one man (see p. 45); and it is not impossible that they may have been suggested by some ritual similar to the continental debates of Summer and Winter. Whoever associated the poem XXVI with XXIX in the Rawlinson MS. B 502 may have done so on this analogy, consciously or otherwise, making Finn and the Lazy Servant sing a poetical contest of Summer against Winter.

This hypothesis of a primitive Celtic seasonal song as part of the Summer and Winter festivals accounts very well for the form and content of the Irish and Welsh poems announcing the new season, but it is very poorly supported by

[1] See *An Seanchaidhe Muimhneach* (Irish Folklore Institute, Dublin, 1932), pp. 326 ff.
[2] Gwynn Jones, *Welsh Folklore and Folk-custom* (Methuen, 1930), p. 154.
[3] Chotzen, *Recherches*, p. 84.

external evidence. Other explanations are perhaps possible. We have seen that nature-gnomic poetry is a way of expressing observance of nature; and though there are practically no true nature gnomes in Irish literature, such a gnomic awareness may still have existed in Ireland as well as in Wales and have been expressed in both languages in ways other than gnomic. Seasonal changes throughout the year are one of the most obvious features in external nature, and most important to a peasant civilisation; gnomic observation under these circumstances might well tend to take the form almost of calendars and describe the seasons or even the individual months in order. The passage from the Cotton Gnomes, quoted on p. 133, shows how the Anglo-Saxon poet classified the seasons; the four Irish poems, XXXI A–D, are almost gnomic poems on the seasons; and the Welsh Verses of the Months (K), though late, may derive from an ancient tradition by which nature gnomes were composed about each month of the year in turn.[1] It may be then that the Irish seasonal poems are the expression of this gnomic awareness turned into pure nature description;[2] XXXI A–D would represent an intermediate stage. Compare Hesiod's *Works and Days*, ll. 582–8:

When the artichoke flourishes and the shrill cicada sitting on the tree pours out its piercing song perpetually from under its wings in the wearisome season of summer, then are goats fattest and wine at its best and women most wanton, but men most languid, for the dogstar oppresses head and knees and the flesh is dry with heat.

Allowing for the differences of climate, flora and fauna, the Irish poets took stock of their seasons in a somewhat

---

[1] Compare a poem in Peniarth MS. 102, f. 8, beginning *Kalangauaf yw henoeth* (rhyme in *-oeth*) which has verses beginning *Calan* for each month, and is in part at least very early.

[2] See p. 127.

similar way, although they chose to record it as a pure description: "The weak white cotton-grass flourishes", "The corncrake clacks, a strenuous bard", "Stags assemble, ravens flourish", "The maiden flourishes in her fine strong prime". The most useful of these gnomic characterisations would be those that foretell and describe a new season, and they are not uncommon in the *Works and Days* in its function as a rudimentary almanac:

But of a different nature is voyaging in the spring for men, when first the leaves appear on the topmost bough as big as the print made by a crow's tread, for then the sea is passable (ll. 678–81).

Such ways of telling when any season has come can easily be collected into a calendar or almanac, as in effect Hesiod does; he indicates the date of the winter ploughing season thus (ll. 448–51):

Take heed likewise when you hear the voice of the crane from the clouds above giving its yearly scream, for it brings the signal for ploughing and announces the season of rainy winter.

The first cry of the cuckoo is the sign of spring rain (ll. 486–9):

When the cuckoo first calls among the oak leaves and rejoices mortals over the boundless earth, then Zeus will rain within three days and cease not, neither overflowing the hoof-print of an ox nor failing to fill it.

The first swallow is another omen of spring (ll. 568–9):

And after that the shrill-crying swallow, daughter of Pandion, arises into the daylight for mankind at the first beginning of Spring.

So in the British Isles, bird song was associated with certain times and days of the year. The calendar of the pseudo-Bede in an early twelfth-century Durham manuscript[1] has under February 12th the entry *Hic aves cantare incipiunt*, and under June 5th, *Hic aves desinunt cantare*. In Bodleian MS. Douce 270, of the thirteenth century, possibly also of Durham origin, the birds commence to sing on February 12th and cease on June 17th. Harley MS. 1804, a fifteenth-century Durham book, gives them as beginning on February 12th. The Red Book of Darley, Corpus Christi MS. 422, written at Winchester in the eleventh century, has a calendar believed to have originated from Sherborne; and under February 11th, *her onginnað fugelas to singenne*, "Now the birds begin to sing"; they are noted as ceasing on June 5th. There is an early Irish poem on the bird cries throughout the year,[2] and Dr Flower remarks[3] of this, "There must surely be some connection between these two traditions" (the English and Irish); "at Durham and Sherborne Irish influence is possible.... It is obviously an old pre-conquest tradition". The Irish poem tells how:

The birds of the world, power without ill, it is to welcome the sun at the nones of January whatever the hour that their flock[4] calls from the dark wood.

On the eighth of the calends of glorious April the swallows come to their pure assembly.... On the eighth of the calends of October what hides them?[5]

At the festival of Ruadán, no trifling saying, it is then that their fetters are unloosed; on the seventeenth of the calends of May the cuckoo calls from the tangled wood.

At the nones of July the birds cease to sing the music of holy days... for Máelruain of Tallaght.

[1] Durham Cathedral Library, Hunter MS. 100 (cf. Migne, *Patr. Lat.* xc, 761–2, 769–70). I owe this and the following details from English MSS. to the kindness of Dr Robin Flower.
[2] Ed. and tr. R. I. Best and H. J. Lawlor, *The Martyrology of Tallaght* (London, 1931), pp. 94 ff.
[3] By letter.
[4] Reading *uar...a sluag*.
[5] I.e. "Why do they leave then?"

At the festival of Ciaran son of the carpenter wild geese come over the cold sea; at the festival of Cyprian, a mighty counsel, the red stag bells from the brown plain.

Six thousand fair years is the world's age without sorrow; sea will burst over every place at the end of the night at the call of the birds.

The birds perform sweet music to the King of cloudy heaven, praising the glorious King; listen to the chorus of the birds from afar.

These bird-song calendars are one way in which the passing of the seasons was noted in the almanac literature of these islands at an early period. Another seasonal presage is the rising of stars and the lengthening and shortening of days; Hesiod marks the end of winter by the rising of Arcturus (*Works and Days*, 564-7):

When Zeus brings to an end the sixty wintry days after the solstice, then the star of Arcturus leaving the sacred stream of Ocean first appears glittering just before dusk.

So an Irish poet reckons the passing of the year by the length of the days:[1]

The day increases in pleasant manner and the night lessens from the festival of fair-flanked Thomas in the East to the festival of dumb Faolán.

The night increases, it is no lie, and every long day diminishes, from the festival of Faolán, look forward, to the festival of Thomas once more.

At the festival of mighty Benedict on the 12th Kal. April, that is the festival you compute, it is no lie, which is of equal length both day and night.

An Irish poem[2] *When to gather herbs*, a little almanac for

---

[1] The poem *In lá oc sínud suairc in mod*, Leabhar Breacc, f. 102, at the end of the December entries of the Félire of Oengus.

[2] Ed. and tr. R. Flower, *Eriu*, IX, pp. 61-8 (fr. B.M. Add. 30512). Perhaps twelfth century.

herbalists, likewise associates the world of nature with the progress of the calendar:

From the 8th Kal. of glorious April to the 3rd Kal. of perfect July, at that time, it is no great contention, it is the top of every herb that heals.

From the 8th Kal. of July after that to the 3rd Kal. October, the stalk of every herb, a deed without prohibition, it is that which heals every distress.

The root of every herb, it is true, from the 8th Kal. October, Diancecht ordained it in his wisdom, to the 8th Kal. of noble April.

Three hundred and sixty-five herbs, that is their number, it is no great untruth, the herbs of every sickness, verses tell of it; let them all be plucked on the 8th Kalends.

The first two of these calendar poems evidently derive their form from the early ecclesiastical martyrologies, which are almanacs of hagiological matter sometimes in verse. The best known is the ninth-century poem called the Félire of Oengus, a poem-list of saints' days throughout the year dated in the Latin way by Calends, Ides and Nones. Some later Welsh prose calendars give the saints' days together with a few notices on the position of the sun in the zodiac.[1] The poems on the bird cries and on the length of days are as it were variations on these, and their clerical origin is unmistakable; the herbalist's poem is in a different class, but the system of dating by Calends (which appears also in the Annals) comes ultimately from learned Latin and therefore ecclesiastical usage. An Anglo-Saxon poem called the *Menologium*, found at the beginning of the Cotton MS. of the Anglo-Saxon Chronicle,[2] shows an interesting development; though not strictly hagiological it recounts the various events of the year, with the important difference from the

[1] E.g. a fifteenth-century calendar in B.M. Add. 14912.
[2] Ed. Plummer, *Two Saxon Chronicles*, I, pp. 273 ff.

other ecclesiastic almanacs whose object it is simply to record dates, that it elaborates its mention of certain seasons with passages of nature poetry not unlike the Athirne and Amorgein poems, nos. XXXI A–D. So from the March and May entries, ll. 29–35 and 75–79, 87–92:

So too it is well known that its Calends come at the end of five days to folk in every place, to nobles and commons, except when the leap-year day occurs in the fourth year, when it comes later by one night to our dwellings, decked with frost; grim March, noisy and glorious, fares among hail-showers.

So soon comes fairly gliding mighty May to cities, gentle and smooth in beauteous array, to woods and plants, splendidly to our dwellings; everywhere it brings forth needful things among the multitude....So it is that at the end of the first week all but one day summer brings to men sun-bright days to their dwellings, warm seasons, when the fields soon blossom with flowers; so joy awakens throughout the world.

The whole style of these passages is quite typical of Anglo-Saxon poetry, secular or religious, and in particular of those poems such as the elegies where allusions to nature occur. For example, a description from an elegy of coming spring and the urge to seafaring that it awakens:

> *Bearwas blostmum nimað, byrig faegriað,*
> *wongas wlitigað, woruld onetteð;*
> *ealle þa gemoniað modes fusne*
> *sefan to siðe, þam þe swa þenceð.*[1]

The woods take on blossom, mansions grow fair, fields become gay, the world is astir; all these things urge on the heart of a high-spirited man to travel, if he be so minded.

The gnomic passage on the seasons quoted on p. 133 is even closer in style; the writer of the *Menologium*, a learned man

---

[1] *The Seafarer*, ll. 48–51, ed. and tr. N. Kershaw, *Anglo-Saxon and Norse Poems*, pp. 22–3.

and presumably a cleric, was clearly ornamenting his rather dull calendar with descriptions imitated from the native poetic tradition.

This view, that the source for the seasonal poems is a native interest in the progress of the seasons and their signs combined with a calendar form derived from learned Latin tradition, seems in itself more probable and much more in accordance with accepted theories about literary origins than the hypothesis of primitive Celtic seasonal celebrations. However, there is little independent evidence that such a native interest existed, at least in Ireland where the seasonal poems are most developed.[1] The likeness to the ecclesiastical and other calendar poems is deceptive, and where such likeness exists the learned poets are more likely to have borrowed from the seasonal poems than the seasonal poets from the calendars. For example, the composer of the *Menologium* elaborated one or two passages in his almanac with nature descriptions adapted from the native elegiac and gnomic tradition. If a poem such as no. XXV were developed out of almanac literature one would expect to find in it the fundamental interest in the calendar for the whole year and the learned method of dating by Calends, Ides and Nones. Or if we suppose that nature poetry arose by isolating and elaborating descriptions of nature in the

[1] There is a calendar poem, ed. and tr. K. Meyer, *Hibernica Minora*, p. 49, dealing with the four great festivals of native Irish observance and not specifically ecclesiastic; but there is no mention of nature in it or of the seasons as such. It goes:

"I relate to you, a surpassing festival, the privileged dues of Bealtain; beer, roots, mild whey, and fresh curds to the fire.

Lugnassad, tell of its dues of every distant year, trial of every glorious fruit, food of herbs on Lugnassad day.

Meat, beer, nut mast, chitterlings, they are the dues of Samhain; a merry bonfire on the hill, buttermilk, fresh-buttered bread.

Trial of every food in order, this is proper at Imbolc; washing of hand and foot and head; it is thus I relate."

religious almanacs, such as the last two verses of the Irish poem on the birds, some kind of religious lyric might be expected much more like poem no. IV than no. XXV and the rest where there are no references to religion. The use of the word *Kalan* in the Welsh poems is no argument for derivation from learned calendars, for the word was borrowed into Welsh in the Romano-British period,[1] just as in the continental May songs where *Kalendas Mayas* and *Chalenda Maia* come from the popular Latin of Roman Gaul. In the Irish seasonal poems only native terms for the seasons are found, *céttamain, sam, gam*, as we should expect; it is in the ecclesiastical almanac literature alone that *Kalann* occurs. Even in the Welsh nature poems the beginning of summer is called by a native word, *kyntefin*.

Another possible source of influence is to be noted, literature about the weather. I have tried to show elsewhere[2] that there was an old Irish genre of prophecy in which prognostications in short phrases about the seasons, weather, fertility and prosperity were given in an early chant-metre. An example that concerns us closely is the prophecy of Néde,[3] who says:

> Good tidings (*scéla*),
> Sea fruitful,
> Strand wave-washed,
> Woods smile,
> Witchcraft flees,
> Orchards prosper,
> Cornfields flourish,
> Bee-swarms abundant,
> The world cheerful,
> Joyous peace,
> Happy summer....

[1] See Loth, *Les Mabinogion*, I, p. 109, note 1.
[2] "Tradition in Early Irish Prophecy", *Man*, XXXIV (May, 1934), p. 67.
[3] Ed. and tr. Wh. Stokes, RC, XXVI, p. 32.

In all these prophecies the shortness of the lines brings about a shortness of phrasing, such as noun + predicative adjective or noun + preposition + noun, or noun + noun in the genitive, with regular omission of the substantive verb. For example, *muir toirthech*, "sea fruitful"; *sam fliuch*, "summer wet"; *sam cin blátha*, "summer without flowers"; *terc ass*, "milk scarce". This reminds us of poem XXVII, a winter poem; it is in a different kind of metre, derived from Latin, but even so the short arrangement of phrases and regular omission of the substantive verb are very similar to the form of prophecies; the phrase *ruirthech rian*, "sea flowing high", suggests *trácht ruirthech*, "strand wave-washed", in Néde's poem; and most significantly it begins and ends with the word *scél*, "tidings", just as Néde's poem does. This phrase *scél lem duib* was clearly a regular convention in Irish as the opening phrase of a prophetic poem[1] and perfectly in place there, though it is hardly an obvious idea in a descriptive poem. Hence no. XXVII seems to be a link between the prophecies and the seasonal poetry; it is itself almost certainly a seasonal poem, not a prophecy, but it seems to have been strongly influenced in its phrasing by the prophetic poems. The difference is not great in any case, for the fragment of Néde's poem quoted could easily be turned into a descriptive summer poem if it were taken as a mere description instead of an augury. The summer poem no. XXV seems even to quote from Néde or at least to use a phrase that appears also in his poem—verse 11, l. 4, *sid subach sam*, "A joyous peace (is) summer", can hardly be independent of Néde's *sid subach, sam sogar*, "joyous peace, happy summer". Perhaps it was a current prophetic or descriptive phrase.

[1] Cf. *Tradition in Early Irish Prophecy*, p. 68; and a prophetic poem in the *Battle of Magh Léana* (ed. and tr. O'Curry, Dublin, 1855, p. 122) beginning *Sgéal leam dhaoibh*.

A different kind of weather and fertility augury known in Ireland (and Wales) is the prose almanac associated with the name of Ezra.[1] They foretell the character of the seasons and other matters, and are derived from mediaeval Latin sources; they base their auguries on the day of the week of the first of January, which is referred to as the *calend*. Phrases like "Winter hard, dry, mournful"[2] may perhaps be echoed in lines such as "Winter...rough, black, dark, misty", in the winter poem no. XXXI B. Another prophecy of similar Latin origin is seen in a tenth-century Irish poem[3] foretelling fertility and prosperity or the reverse according to the winds which blow on the calends of January.

All these weather prognostications may have helped to mould the phrasing of some of our seasonal poems, and perhaps the form of one, but they cannot be looked on as in any way their origin.

The question of authorship remains. It has usually been assumed[4] that the Irish seasonal poems are the work of hermits and all part of the hermit literature, because the real character of hermit poetry has not been defined. But the hermits scarcely mention the seasons and there is no reason to think that they were particularly interested in them, while the essential characteristics of hermit poetry described in Chapter I are entirely absent in the seasonal

---

[1] See my article "The Auguries of Esdras concerning the Character of the Year", *Bull.* VII, pp. 5 ff.

[2] *Op. cit.* p. 12.

[3] Ed. and tr. K. Meyer, *Hibernica Minora*, pp. 39–41.

[4] G. Murphy, in *Studies*, March, 1931, pp. 87 ff., assuming that the source for *all* Irish nature poetry was religious, supposes that the seasonal poetry was *paganised*; but even so—and this is most unlikely in itself—the hermit poetry could not have developed into the seasonal, the differences are too great. Yet the seasonal poets may have known the hermit poems and felt their influence.

poems. The personal tone, too, which gives the hermit poems their unity, is lacking; contrast no. I or II with no. XXV—the last is a disjointed catalogue of delightful images, not the same vital whole as the song of Manchín for example; it lacks style. The following phrases in the same poem tell against the hermit theory: "Man thrives, the maiden flourishes in her fine strong prime", "Strong is the †   † of the swift warrior", "A mad ardour upon you to race horses, the ranked host is ranged around". Hermits were not interested in horse-racing and flourishing maidens. Again in the Athirne poems, XXXI A, "there is occupation then for everyone", said of autumn, suggests harvesting or some such communal work not part of the solitary's existence. Nos. XXV–XXVI are written in a curiously irregular and unusual style like an adaptation of the syllabic metres to the earlier native *retoric*, which suggests that the poet was deliberately archaising and therefore aware of an older tradition of seasonal poetry, unless this is simply another case of influence from the prophecies. In any case it contrasts with the hermit poems which are always in regular metres and show no tendency to archaise. We have seen (p. 43) how five of the seasonal poems were attributed to Finn mac Cumaill or given a Fenian situation, how of the four of these that had a context three clearly did not belong to it, and how there was almost nothing in any of them to show that they were Fenian poems; indeed, they mostly date from a time when the Fenian cycle was only beginning to take shape. It is natural to suppose that the attribution was made on the strength of the general likeness in scene—outdoor life—between them and the genuine Fenian poetry (see Chapter II). Finn mac Cumaill was always famous as a prophet and seer;[1] this and the coincidence with Finn File,

[1] Cf. C. Plummer, *Bethada Naém nErenn*, I, p. 192, where he is called "chief sage and prophet of Ireland".

"Finn the Poet", traditionally king of Leinster and ancestor of the Leinster kings, may have induced the scribes to count as the work of Finn mac Cumaill any poems of unknown authorship which they thought vaguely similar to others known to belong to the Fenian group. The attribution at least implies that it had not occurred to them to connect the seasonal poems with the hermits or the saints. Its real significance may be that the poems were transmitted and even composed by the same class of author as those that put together the Fenian tales. These authors were not clerics, nor were they official bards of the type who earlier composed such works as the genealogical poems[1] and the various royal eulogies; they were probably a kind of story-teller, like the Welsh *cyfarwyddiaid* who composed the Mabinogion and the Llywarch Hen elegies. Perhaps the compositions in very early Irish literature (that is, made definitely before the Middle Irish period) most similar to the seasonal poetry on general grounds are the two poems in the Voyage of Bran.[2] In style there is the same lack of general form combined with the same sensuous imagery; and so far as it is possible to trace any particular social *milieu* in the seasonal poems, they seem to agree. "A mad ardour upon you to race horses, the ranked host is ranged around" would appeal to the same class and circle as the Bran poems with their "glorious range ...the plain on which the hosts hold games" and the "many steeds on its surface"; that is, perhaps, the same class of society to whom the sagas were favourites, the secular upper classes. Their poets, perhaps a lower class than those who sang the genealogies and eulogies, would be in touch with both the native tradition and the learned,[3] and in a position

---

[1] Ed. K. Meyer, *Ueber die aelteste Irische Dichtung*, Berlin, 1913–14.
[2] Ed. and tr. K. Meyer (Nutt, London, 1895).
[3] Cf. the mixed classical and folk-tale references and themes in a work like the *Feast of Bricriu*.

to combine them; to draw on the popular songs sung at seasonal festivals, if such existed, and the almanacs of weather augury and weather and fertility prophecies. Three or four centuries later such poets would be telling Fenian stories and singing Fenian poems to the descendants of the people who listened to the Voyage of Bran and to the seasonal songs. In Wales, the same class of people would be hearing the same seasonal themes from the same kind of poets, who for these and for their gnomic and elegiac poems used the characteristic early englyn metre.

The ultimate source for seasonal poetry in Ireland and Wales may be no more than a general interest in the phenomena of the seasons rather like but distinct from the interest implied in the nature-gnomic poetry, but the very definite genre of seasonal announcement seems to demand some more specific explanation; various theories to account for it have been advanced and queried in this chapter.

CHAPTER V

PROBLEMS OF WELSH NATURE POETRY[1]

The reader's first reaction to early Welsh nature poetry is one of disappointment. He is pleased with the setting, with the mountain snow and the tops of the ash trees, but only puzzled and annoyed by the unfamiliar gnomes. He avoids the difficulty by forcing these to fit the context[2] and by laying all the stress on the nature setting; that is, he persuades himself that they are really true nature poems which lapse occasionally into regrettable trivialities. Or he may take the view that the nature passages are a debased reminiscence of a school of nature poetry once flourishing, a "re-hash of better stuff"[3] which somehow and with miserable lack of poetic genius got joined on to those "sententious irrelevancies", the human gnomes; and that "Mountain Snow" and the other formulae are meaningless preambles designed to aid the memory in the recitation of proverbs. It is easy to solve such problems by saying that the poets were so incompetent as to know no better, but poetical conventions do not come about in that way, and a convention so marked and so persistent as that of the Welsh seasonal passages must surely have arisen from something more permanent. Obviously enough, seasonal descriptive poetry and gnomic poetry are not on the face of it good companions, and it is

[1] The remarks about nature poetry in this chapter refer only to nature descriptions and not to nature gnomes (which have been discussed in Chapter III); that is, to the quasi-gnomic poetry.

[2] "On Winter's Day a secret shared is fine" (cf. Sieper, *Die Altenglische Elegie*, p. 69) and so on.

[3] G. Davies, *The Welsh Bard*, p. 88.

one of the objects of this study to find out how they came together.

Actually there is nothing to show that there was ever a school of highly mature nature poetry in Wales before the period of our poems, in the sense in which the Irish seasonal poems are mature. We have seen that the Welsh poems, like the Irish, may be based rather on a somewhat rudimentary or even popular poetry about the seasons and the times of year and the weather. But it has sometimes been assumed that the Welsh seasonal poetry, poem B for example, was borrowed from the Irish, and the assumption is superficially a natural one. It is known that there was a fine nature poetry in Ireland already in the ninth century; certain supposed resemblances made it seem that there was some interinfluence, and the superiority of the Irish poetry suggested that it was from that side—"the only discernible probability of initiative in nature poetry is in Irish".[1] It was supposed, for example, that the sketchy "impressionistic" phrasing in Welsh was taken from the Irish; but on the contrary the Irish poems do full syntactical justice to every thought, and in particular the characteristic Welsh omission of the substantive verb in phrases like *bas ryt*, "The ford (is) shallow" (H, 12, iii), which increases this sketchy appearance, is almost unknown in Irish. There is one exception, the poem XXVII, which has sometimes been quoted as a parallel to B, but we have proposed a different explanation for this (p. 171). It is true that the Irish poems do consist of short and rather unconnected descriptive sentences, but so for that matter do the mediaeval Latin spring poems and English songs like *Sumer is icumen in*; the following quotation from a second-century Chinese poem[2] shows that short

[1] Glyn Davies, *The Welsh Bard*, p. 93.
[2] Arthur Waley, 170 *Chinese Poems* (Constable Miscellany, 1928), p. 48.

descriptive phrases are just what might occur independently in various literatures as a means of characterising a season by glimpses of its more notable features:

> Autumn wind rises; white clouds fly;
> grass and trees wither; geese go south;
> orchids all in bloom; chrysanthemums smell sweet.

This is remarkably like the Irish seasonal poems, but here at least there can be no suggestion of borrowing.[1] Other causes may have helped to emphasise the "impressionistic" effect. The early Welsh poems have a strong inclination to sententious and even epigrammatic phrasing,[2] not only in the gnomes; and no doubt this tendency to brief expression is as much responsible for the phrasing *caun barywhaud*, "bearded the grass" (B, 4, ii), a nature description, as for *carcharaór dall*, "a prisoner the blind" (H, 14, iii), a gnome. The englyn metre is one which lends itself to division into three semi-independent lines and therefore short phrases (see below), and the first line of the type called englyn *penfyr* also divides easily into two halves. Thus the "sketchy" style attributed to Irish influence can be accounted for as a natural way of describing a season, heightened by a native brevity in expression and by the peculiar character of the englyn metre. The first lines of poems XXV and A, *céttamain caín re* and *kintevin keinhaw amsser*, have been taken as a case of Welsh nature poetry borrowing an Irish stock spring-beginning; but it is probably a coincidence. The words *cyntefin* and *cein* are common enough in early Welsh poetry, but the phrase *céttamain caín* only occurs in this one place in the Irish poems. The accepted theory as to how the

[1] When the Welsh nature poetry is not seasonal but for example elegiac, the independent phrase treatment is not so noticeable; e.g. C, verse 10, where the englyn is a syntactical whole.

[2] Cf. as an example of putting conversation in a gnomic way, *Nest a dywawd im*... "*Gnawd i dyn dylaw dylif ny gwe*", MA, 207 a, 6–7.

supposed borrowing took place,[1] or rather the view put forward in 1913[2] and not since contradicted (so far as I am aware), is that the early Welsh nature poetry was largely composed by hermits influenced by Irish poems. "There were hermit poets again, if we may piece up Welsh literary history from that of Ireland."[3] But may we? Professor Davies' argument is this: the Irish nature poetry was written by hermits; the Welsh nature poetry is similar in style to the Irish; therefore the Welsh nature poetry was also written by hermits. Actually the similarity if any is with the Irish seasonal, not hermit, poetry; we have seen that the Irish nature poetry is very far from being all the work of hermits, and that the definite characteristics of hermit poetry are absent in much of it and other, different, characteristics present. So with the Welsh; it is impossible to point to anything in the Welsh poetry which could be called characteristic of the hermits, though Professor Davies has attempted to do so. He refers to the poem BBC IX (which contains our extract A) as a proof of hermit origin, particularly the lines

> In hill, in dale, in islands of the sea,
> in every way one goes
> from the blessed Christ there is no seclusion.

Now this poem, if it is not separate from poem A (see p. 76), describes the misery and longing felt by the author in spring time when the loss of his dead friends contrasted with the rejuvenated world strikes him with all the crueller force; and that is not a hermit motif. In any case the hermits

---

[1] E.g. C. O'Rahilly, *Ireland and Wales*, p. 127: "It does not seem an altogether improbable conjecture that these Irish monks and clerics should have taught their brother-Celts in Wales that love of nature which we find expressed in these fragmentary poems" (the Welsh gnomic and quasi-gnomic poems).

[2] Glyn Davies, *The Welsh Bard*.

[3] Glyn Davies, ZCP, XVII, p. 127.

sought closer communion with Christ, not seclusion from him. The lines quoted mention, it is true, islands, which were a favourite spot for hermitages, but I think "In hill", etc. means simply "everywhere", and the thought is that Christ is all-pervading. Compare these lines from an *alba* by the twelfth-century Provençal poet Uc de la Bachélerie:[1]

> *En mar, en plan, ni en roca,*
> *non puesc ad Amor gandir.*

On sea, on plain, nor among the rocks, I cannot escape from love.

Professor Davies is not very clear as to what hermit characteristics are. He tries to show that the Irish nature poetry was not written by hunters or farmers, who he assumes did not live in comfort, but by hermits, who he believes did do so; and he quotes poem XXX, verse 7, l. 1, "Snug is our cauldron upon its hook", as evidence of the "physical comfort without which these poems could hardly have come into being".[2] But the Irish hermit poetry and hagiological literature show that comfort is the last thing that a hermit desired or wrote about. We have seen Coemgen at Glendaloch on his stony bed (p. 99), and many similar instances could be produced.[3] A love of natural beauty is a very different thing from a love of comfort, which an Irish hermit would have thought positively immoral, nor did he regard his "little hut in the wilderness" at all in the spirit of our modern romantic "Lake Isle of Innisfree". The whole theory of Welsh poet-hermits under Irish influence is based on a false analogy unsupported by internal evidence.

[1] Appel, *Prov. Chrest.*, 5th ed., p. 92, ll. 23–4.
[2] *Welsh Bard*, etc., p. 92. In any case the speaker of poem XXX is not the poet in person, and the remark is very natural in the circumstances of the poem. No conclusion can possibly be drawn from it as to the comfort or otherwise of the actual poet's circumstances.
[3] Cf. Gougaud, *Les Chrétientés Celtiques* (Paris, 1911), chap. 3, § 12 (pp. 96 ff.), "La Vie Ascetique".

As for external evidence, there is nothing to show that the early Welsh hermits were interested in nature poetry, any more than the Irish hermits were before the ascetic movement of Maelruain. In short, Welsh literature is in the same position as regards hermit nature poetry as Irish would have been in but for the Tallaght movement—it does not exist.

Still less is Irish poetry responsible for the curious jumble of genres that make up a poem like E.

> Mountain snow; red are the tops of the pear trees;
> fierce and serried are spears;
> alas for longing, my brothers! (verse 21)

This is a case where four different kinds of poetry are brought together in one englyn; "Mountain snow" is a seasonal nature statement, "Red are the tops of the pear trees" a quite unconnected nature gnome, "Fierce and serried are spears" a human gnome, and "Alas for longing, my brothers!" still another element proper neither to gnomic nor to seasonal poetry, where someone appears to be speaking about himself. The last is not accounted for at all by Professor Davies' theory of the "nature tagged maxim", yet lines like it are not uncommon in quasi-gnomic poetry. Any hypothesis designed to explain the Welsh "contamination" must take them into account.

The two chief kinds of stanza used in our Welsh poems are called the Englyn Milwr and the Englyn Penfyr. The milwr consists of three rhyming lines of seven syllables; for example D, 1:

> *Bagla6c bydin, bag6y onn,*
> *hwyeit yn llynn, graenwynn tonn,*
> *trech no chant kyssul callon.*

The penfyr has normally a first line of ten syllables, a second of six, and a third of seven; the second and third lines rhyme with the seventh, eighth or ninth syllable of the first, thus isolating a phrase (called the *gair cyrch*) of three, two or one syllables at the end of the first line, whose last syllable may rhyme internally with the second line or is at any rate *metrically* (but *not* in phrasing) closely connected with the second line. For example, H, 33:

    10. Gorwyn blaen ysga6; hyd(y)r ana6 | unic;
    6. gna6t y dreissic dreissya6;
    7. g6ae a d6c daffar o la6.

This stanza might be printed

Gorwyn blaen ysga6; hydyr ana6 | unic; gna6t y dreissic dreissya6;
    g6ae a d6c daffar o la6,

which indicates the (incomplete) metric unity of the first two lines as against the third; but it is an extremely clumsy way of arrangement, and shows by its own top-heaviness that the penfyr cannot really be in origin a verse of one short and one long line. However, that is beside the point at issue, which is that often but by no means always the first two lines of a penfyr do form a unity of phrase as against the third—RBH, 1045, 2-3:

    Stavell Gyndylan ys tywyll | heno,
    heb dan, heb gannwyll;
    namyn Du6 p6y am dyry p6yll?

The hall of Cynddylan is dark | to-night, without fire, without candle; who but God will preserve my reason?

The tendency is naturally one which would be encouraged in the elegies, with their strong leaning to epigrammaticism and contrast. The last line is able to give the point to a verse in which the first two lines were an introductory preface; and the englyn is very comparable in this to the Greek and Latin elegiac couplet. In much the same way the first two lines of englynion, whether milwr or penfyr, may be used in the dialogues to carry an address to the interlocutor while the third line contains the real point of the remark. E.g. BBC, f. xlix b, 15–16:

> *Ath kiuarchaw, hv yscun gur,*
> *ae iscuid in aghen;*
> *pebir gur, pan iv dy echen?*

I address you, daring and hardy man, with your shield ready at need; bold man, whence is your lineage?

BBC, f. li, 16,–f. li b, 1:

> *Y gur nim guelas beunit*
> *y tebic y gur deduit,*
> *ba hid ei dy a phan doit?*

Friend, who have not seen me every day, who are like to a prosperous man, where are you going and whence do you come?

Again, in the *Englynion y Clyweit* the first two lines of each englyn are a sort of preface giving the name of the speaker and often the circumstances, and the last line is the gnome which he pronounces; the preface is generally without much significance, chosen simply for the rhyme with the last line, and it is obvious that each stanza was composed around the "sting", the gnome of the third line. E.g. verse 15,

> *A glyweisti a gant Padarn,*
> *pregethwr kywir kadarn?*
> *"A wnel dyn, Duw ae barn."*

Hast thou heard what St Padarn sang, a strong and trusty preacher? "What is done by man is judged by God."

None the less englynion like these are a whole, with just that element of counterpoise which makes a finished and effective piece of work.

Often, however, the englyn is not a thought-unity at all. This is a type of great importance to our poems, the verse where the first two lines appear to have no connection with the third or with the poem as a whole. For example, from a dialogue:[1]

> Gwalchmei: *Abrwysg vydd tonn aneddfawl*
> *pan fo mor yn y kanawl;*
> *pwy wyt, filwr anianawl?*
> Tristan: *Abrwysg fydd tonn a tharan*
> *kyd boed brwysg a gwahan;*
> *ynydd trin mi yw Trystan.*

Gwalchmei: "Huge is the ungovernable wave when the sea is in the midst; who are you, spirited warrior?"
Tristan: "Huge is the wave and the thunder, though it be vigorous and dissimilar; in the day of combat I am Tristan."

Here the irrelevance of the first two lines of each verse, the fact that they are nature poetry, and that they are closely parallel in the two verses, will be noted. Again, poem B, stanza 24, in that part of the poem where a story is being acted by two or more characters:

> *Kinteic guint, creilum coed,*
> *crin caun, caru iscun;*
> *Pelis enuir, pa tir hun?*

The wind is swift, raw and bare is the wood, the reeds are withered, the stag is hardy; wicked Pelis, what land is this?

The two lines of nature poetry actually have no connection with the third, though it may seem at first sight that they have. RBH, 1037, 15–16, from a dialogue,

> *Medal migned, kalet ri6,*
> *rac carn cann tal glann a vri6;*
> *edewit ny wnelher nydi6.*

Soft are the bogs, hard the slope, the edge of the bank breaks under the hoof of the white horse; a promise not performed is none.

Again the first two lines are irrelevant nature poetry. Sometimes in dialogues the first line is an address, the second irrelevant nature poetry, and the third is the point, with a

[1] *Bull.* v, p. 123.

PROBLEMS OF WELSH NATURE POETRY

tendency to parallelism between the three lines of each of a pair of stanzas. E.g.:

> Gwalchmei: *Trystram gyneddfav blaengar,*
> *gorwlyched kafod blaen dar,*
> *tyred imddiddan a'th gar.*
> Tristan: *Gwalchmai gyneddfav gwrthrych,*
> *gorwlyched kafod blaen rrych,*
> *mi af i'r mann i mynych.*[1]

Gwalchmei: "Tristan of ambitious character—the shower wets[2] the top of the oak—come and talk with your kinsman."
Tristan: "Gwalchmei of plain character—the shower wets[2] the top of the furrow—I will go wherever you wish."

Still another type is where the first line of an englyn milwr is irrelevant and the second and third contain the point—RBH, 1037, 39–42:

> *Tonn tyruit, toit eruit,*
> *pan ant kyurein y govit*
> *G6en, g6ae ryhen o' th etlit.*
>
> *Ton tyruit, toit aches,*
> *pan ant kyfrein y neges*
> *G6en, g6ae ryhen ryth golles.*

The wave †is tumultuous†, it covers †the strand†; when warriors go out to battle, Gwen, woe to the old man who grieves for thee.

The wave †is tumultuous†, it covers the flood; when warriors go on their business, Gwen, woe to the old man who has lost thee.

Here again the parallelism is very marked.

RBH, 1026, 14–17:

> Llywelyn: *Eiry mynyd, gwynt am ty;*
> *kanys llefery uelly,*
> *beth, 6rnerth, a wna hynny?*
> Gwrnerth: *Eiry mynyd, g6ynt deheu,*
> *kanys traethaf prif eiryeu,*
> *tebyckaf y6 mae angheu.*

---

[1] *Bull.* v, p. 124.   [2] Reading *gorwlychid*.

Llywelyn: "Mountain snow, wind about the house; since you say so, what is it, Gwrnerth, that causes that?"

Gwrnerth: "Mountain snow, wind in the south; since I will pronounce a weighty saying, it is most likely it is death."

Here then is a type of englyn where in a dialogue or story only part of a verse, mostly the third line, has anything to do with the "plot", and the rest seems to be nature poetry that is quite beside the mark; and the type, since it occurs in the Llywarch elegies, is at least as old as the ninth century.

But this formula is precisely the same as that which has been the puzzle in the quasi-gnomic poems, such verses as D, 8:

Gla6 allan, g6lychyt redyn,
g6ynn gro mor, goror ewyn;
tec a gann6yll p6yll y dyn.

Compare the verse quoted above:

Medal migned, kalet ri6,
rac carn cann tal glann a vri6;
edewit ny wnelher nydi6.

The context shows that the second of these stanzas is to be taken as part of a dialogue, and that Llywarch's wife is taunting their son Gwen with boasting;[1] but without its context the verse might very well be one of a quasi-gnomic series like the "Rain outside" series of poem D. Indeed the third line which in its proper context is a taunt in gnomic form appears as a pure gnome as the third line of Engl. Clyw. st. 18, and also in Pen. 17, prov. 265 and MA, 844 b, 25.

Does this mean that when in dialogue and elegy a speaker is made to quote a current gnome he does so in the form it took in contemporary quasi-gnomic poetry, that is, a whole verse whose first two lines were descriptive nature poetry and the third line the human gnome in question? If so, the problem of the quasi-gnomic stanza would be no nearer a solution. We have seen, however, that this same irrelevance

---

[1] Ifor Williams, *The Poems of Llywarch Hen*, p. 17.

occurs in dialogues when the third line cannot be a gnome, for example in the Tristan and Gwalchmei verses on p. 184. Clearly, verses with two lines of "irrelevant" nature poetry and a gnomic third line (that is, quasi-gnomic verses) must be treated as parallel to verses such as these where the two "irrelevant" lines of nature poetry are followed by a third line which is not gnomic; and the two kinds doubtless arose in the same way. It has been shown how the englyn has an inherent tendency to fall apart into groups, most usually of 2+1 lines, or sometimes of 1+2; and further, that the first group, once as it were a real preface to the "point", could become more and more disconnected until it was entirely irrelevant. It is safe to conclude in this way that the "irrelevant" nature poetry just illustrated in dialogues and quasi-gnomic poems must be a development from a stage when the nature-beginning was *not* irrelevant. By the gradual falling apart of what was at first a poetic unity there must have arisen in time the fixed conventional formula seen in these quasi-gnomic and dialogue verses. If it is possible to point to a type of englyn where a "preface" of nature poetry and a third line with the "point" *are* a true thought-unity, the solution of the problem would be a good deal nearer.

Fortunately it is possible. It is not uncommon to find such stanzas in the elegies, where the nature poetry comes in quite relevantly in one or other of the ways mentioned in Chapter II, either as a contrast of a pleasant season with the wretchedness of the speaker, or as a lament on the harshness of weather and surroundings, or as a cry by the exiled or ruined and unfortunate man of how the sad scene fits in with his mood. RBH, 1036, 15–16:

Wooden staff, it is early summer, the furrow is brown, the young corn is curly; it grieves me to look at your crook.[1]

---

[1] See p. 115.

RBH, 1036, 26–7:

†Boisterous† is the wind, white is the hue of the border of the wood, the stag is emboldened, the hill is bleak; feeble is the old man, slowly he moves.[1]

C. 13–14:

Clamorous are the birds, wet is the shingle, the leaves fall, miserable is the exile; I do not deny I am sick to-night.

Clamorous are the birds, wet is the strand, clear is the firmament, extensive the wave; the heart is withered with longing.

The last line of this last verse was actually taken for a gnome in the Myvyrian Archaeology (848 b, 25).

We have already noted (p. 131) how sententious the early elegies are, particularly in the third line of the englyn. These elegiac gnomes are almost all entirely relevant to the verse in which they occur, though a number of them are found as separate gnomes in the later prose collections.[2] The following are found in the Cynddylan elegy, RBH, XVI: *a uynno Du6 derffit, amgeled am vn nydi6, ny elwir coet o un prenn, gwae ny wna da ae dyuyd, gna6t man ar gran kyniuiat, gwae ieueinc a eidun brotre*; in the series of elegies, RBH, XI, *gna6t ffo ar ffraeth, edewit ny wnelher nydi6, ni bu eidyl hen yn was, eidil heb dim digoner*; in the Aber Cuawg elegy, poem C, *g6ell corra6c no chebyd, cof gan ba6p a gar, g6y6 callon rac hiraeth, nyt eidun detwyd dyhed, ny chel grud kystud callon, ny at Du6 da y diryeit, nyt atwna Du6 ar a wnel, cas dyn yman y6 cas Du6 vry*.

Now the dialogues, or at least such dialogues as that in RBH, XI, are all more or less part of the elegiac englyn tradition, and it would be natural for verses like RBH, 1036,

---

[1] See p. 116.

[2] Compare the Seithennin poem, BBC, ff. liii b–liv, where verses 4–8 end with gnomes which are relevant to their verses but were quoted by themselves in later gnomic collections; the poem is not an elegy but an adaptation of a tale.

26–7, to appear in dialogues no less than in elegies. The step from poem C, verse 14, to RBH, 1037, 15–16 (p. 184), is not great; but nature poetry would be less relevant in a dialogue than in an elegy, and it is probably partly due to this that the split in the unity came about, a split seen already in RBH, 1037, 15–16.[1]

How then did this type become amalgamated with gnomic poetry to form the predominating one in quasi-gnomic poetry? It is quite fair to suppose that it happened in much the same way. The elegies contained verses like RBH, 1036, 26–7, where two lines of relevant nature poetry were followed by a third that could be treated as a gnome; perhaps the gnomic poets incorporated such verses whole in their sententious poetry, and by doing so established the conventional quasi-gnomic formula. They would be all the readier to do this because their own purely gnomic verses often consisted of two lines of nature *gnomes* and one line of human gnome (e.g. poem H, 10). The preface of nature description would then become irrelevant, and the natural tendency of the englyn to split into two independent groups would help the process. Actually there are a number of

[1] The poem B is a good example of this. It is a mixture of pure nature-descriptive verses, verses of nature description and apparently irrelevant gnomes, and others which are all dialogue and story. It is worth suggesting that the first group, pure weather descriptions, may be a development from the elegiac theme, as in the "wooden crook" stanzas, with the personal element omitted. The second group is all concerned with gnomes on cowardice; if Ifor Williams' theory is correct, that this part is a somewhat fragmentary dialogue where one speaker taunts the other with being afraid to go out to battle and the other replies that the weather is too bad (see CLH, p. 176), then the gnomes and nature parts are not irrelevant to each other and the verses stand on the same level as for example the verses C, 13–14. If on the other hand this part is not a dialogue, then it is a quasi-gnomic series of the same type as poem D, where it will be noticed one stanza, no. 9, is itself "irrelevant" nature poetry with a third line on cowardice.

verses in the quasi-gnomic poems which might as well belong to dialogue or elegy—RBH, 1037, 15–16 (p. 184) is an example of a verse from an elegiac dialogue which could very well have come from quasi-gnomic poetry. There are also lines in which as we saw (p. 181) a personal element is introduced which is quite foreign both to pure descriptive nature poetry and to gnomic poetry. Examples are H, 9, iii, "Thought is valiant; care has been long in my heart"; *ibid.* 19, ii, "Flowing are my tears to-day"; E, 6, iii–iv, "Though a tale be told me, I recognise shame where it is"; *ibid.* 21, iii, "Oh for longing, my brothers"; *ibid.* 26, ii–iii, "Strong is my arm and my shoulder, I pray I may not be a hundred years old"; *ibid.* 33, ii, "Scarcely anything at all interests me". Perhaps such lines as these were brought into quasi-gnomic verse from the elegies along with the descriptive nature poetry and the elegiac gnomes.

The theory will account very well for certain types of quasi-gnomic stanza, most of those in poems D and E for example; but it does not explain the recurrent seasonal openings, the "Winter's Day" phrasing and the rest, which must belong somehow or other to seasonal and calendar poetry.[1] Granted a primitive stereotyped beginning to seasonal-carol verses such as "Winter's Day", "May Day", there must have been some cause for the introduction of gnomes into the season song. It may have come about in the following way. A season carol and descriptive verse like, let us say, "It is Winter's Day, the cattle are thin, the stag is hunched, the oak leaves fall", was felt to be so closely allied to pure nature-gnomic poetry in its descriptive phrases that nature description and nature gnome were confounded and

[1] The "mountain snow" type may be derived from a cowardice plea or some sort of elegiac theme, as suggested above; but this is not a very satisfactory solution for the beginning "Kalan Gaeaf" in spite of the possible parallel with the calendar stanzas on p. 115.

the fusion with the pure nature-cum-gnomic type occurred. Take again a stanza like H, 23:

> Delightful is the top of the grove, of equal height are its trees, and the leaves of the oak tree fall;
> happy is he who sees whom he loves.

The first two lines could be treated as nature descriptions—"(It is autumn), delightful is the top of the grove, its trees are of equal height and the leaves of the oak trees are falling"—or as gnomes, which the analogy of the others shows this stanza as a whole to be—"The top of a grove is delightful, the trees of a grove are of equal height; oak leaves fall". The Verses of the Months (poem K) may have a similar origin, for their seasonal beginnings and nature descriptions, though probably gnomic, can be taken also as pure descriptions ("It is the month of January, the valley is smoky" or "In the month of January the valley is smoky") whichever way we look at them.

Still another explanation of the fusion of gnomic and seasonal verse suggests itself on the analogy of Anglo-Saxon gnomic poetry, where calendar gnomes like "Winter is coldest" are associated with human gnomes like "Truth is most manifest"; and if there were such calendar and seasonal gnomes in primitive Welsh gnomic poetry it might well be a probable one. The gnomic Verses of the Months, in which the seasonal gnomic element could be treated as descriptive, are unfortunately very late, but if they are based on an early poetic type, that type may be the missing link sought for here. That is to say, a calendar-and-human gnomic genre such as *On Winter's Day the berries are hard, leaves are aloft, and the ponds are full; in the morning before setting out woe to him who trusts a stranger*, could be treated as quasi-gnomic, pure seasonal description + gnome, and would then yield the stanza G, 1. This would do away with much of the need for the theory about primitive seasonal song in Wales outlined in Chapter IV.

The solution of these complicated problems is perhaps like this: Either the original seasonal carol was influenced by the ordinary nature-cum-human gnomic poetry to take in a gnomic element; or, a primitive mixture of calendar *gnomic* and human gnomic poetry like the parts of the Cotton Gnomes referred to, was easily taken as seasonal *description* and human gnomic poetry. A rough quasi-gnomic seasonal poetry was produced in either case. Meanwhile a rather different, not seasonal, kind of quasi-gnomic poetry grew up out of the fusion of elegy and gnomic poetry and adopted certain personal elegiac characteristics.[1] The process caused a split in the thought unity of the original gnomic stanza, because taken from its context the elegiac stanza of the type referred to would itself split easily into two unrelated groups of nature and human poetry, and in fact showed a tendency to do this even in the elegies themselves.

[1] Note that the personal element appears in the Verses of the Months, st. 9, l. 3, "Woe to my heart for longing".

NOTE
THE LATER WELSH POETS

The Welsh "Gogynfeirdd", the court bards of the late twelfth to early fourteenth centuries, are outside the scope of this study which is concerned only with the englyn period of the ninth to twelfth centuries; the Gogynfeirdd cannot be called "early" in time or development. However, they cannot be passed over entirely, because their very limited nature poetry has some bearing on the problems of the earlier literature.

The following passages are to be noted. The beginning of an elegy by Einion ab Gwalchmai:[1]

> The season of May, the day is lengthy, it is lawful to make gifts;
> the wood is not inconspicuous, fair is the hue of the grove;
> birds are chattering, tranquil is the sea,
> the waves fall still, the wind fades...
> the solitudes are quiet; it is not for me to be silent.

A poem by Llywarch ab Llywelyn[2] beginning:

> The Calends of October, the length of day lessens,
> the Calends[3] marked by the high moon that lights the path;
> there is commotion in the river-mouths, the sea is in flood,
> winter is imminent, the brine is surging.

A poem by Gwalchmai[4] which begins:

> It is calm summer, tranquil is the sea,
> beautiful is the forest, cool the turf of the grove.

A poem by Dafydd Benfras[5] beginning:

> Delightful is the chill-running foam,
> it is vehement in January, great, sea-pebbly.

---

[1] MA, 230 a; Hendre G. p. 40. [2] MA, 200 b; Hendre G. p. 262.
[3] Reading *calan* for MS. *calaf*. [4] MA, 146 a; Hendre G. p. 28.
[5] MA, 221 b.

The beginning of an elegy, by the same:[1]

It is May, less and less is the flood in the river.

The *Gorhoffedd* or "boasting-poem" is a rambling discourse by the poet about his own emotions. Nature poetry is found in a *gorhoffedd* by Hywel ab Owein Gwynedd in praise of North Wales:[2]

> I love her shores and her mountains
> and her fortress by the wood and her fair lands,
> and her dales and her waters and her valleys,
> and her white seagulls and her fine women;
> I love her soldiers and her docile horses
> and her woods and her strongholds and her dwellings;
> I love her fields and her land with the clover on it....
> A white foaming wave washes the grave,
> a white foaming wave bold against towns
> of the colour of hoarfrost when it rises;
> I love the shore of Meirionydd
> where I was pillowed on a white arm;
> I love the nightingale on the privet of the wood
> at the meeting of the two waters in the valley of prayer....

Gwalchmai's boasting-poem has a number of passages about nature:[3]

The sun rises early, summer hastens on,
pleasant is the chatter of birds, glorious is the glad weather....
(I have watched) the murmuring fords, the waters of Dygen Freiddin,
very green is the untrodden grass, the water is resplendent;
loud is the nightingale that is skilled in song;
seagulls at play on the bosom of the flood,
glistening are their feathers, in noisy parties;
my thoughts are afar in early summer
because of love....

[1] MA, 221 b.   [2] MA, 198 a; Hendre G. p. 315.
[3] MA, 142 b; Hendre G. p. 16.

Tumultuous is the meeting of the waters, ardent is the day,
gentle[1] chant of birds in warbling song....
Delightful is the crest of the apple tree with its clustering flowers,
proud is the surface of the wood....
I love the nightingale of May that hinders morning sleep
with her slow eyes and her long bright face;
I love the splendid deer....
I love the bird with its gentle voice,
the unceasing songster of the wood....
...The green wave at Aber Dau,
it makes for the bright green shore of fair streams;
steadfastly sings the bird,...
pleasant is the untrodden grass when the days increase,
pleasant is the proud surface of the wood of fair blossoms....
Pleasant[2] is early summer, fair, of long days,
tranquil † † of summer, joyous and blest....

It is impossible to discuss here in any detail what was the source of this Gogynfeirdd nature poetry. It cannot have been derived from the englyn poetry as we know it, for the differences of style are too great. Glyn Davies looks for the origin in the "nature-tagged maxim" of the englynion (that is, the quasi-gnomic poems),[3] but nothing so peculiar in the history of Welsh nature poetry as the quasi-gnomic poems can have been the source for the Gogynfeirdd passages; if it were, what has happened to the "maxim"? The second group, the *gorhoffedd* poems, needs no explanation; it is a spontaneous expression of feeling, and as a genre appears to be entirely Welsh.[4] There is nothing to connect it with the englyn poetry. A likeness has been noted with the poem *The Pleasant Things of Taliesin* (see p. 87), which may be

---

[1] Reading *war* for MS. *o ar*.
[2] Reading *aduwyn* with Hendre G.   [3] See pp. 127–8.
[4] Unless *Finn's Delights* (no. XXII) can be regarded as a rudimentary one, but the characteristic boasting is absent there. The French and Provençal *gabs* are not really comparable.

itself a *gorhoffedd*, but its lack of personal feeling and its definitely gnomic tone are against it. The first group consists of nature-beginnings to poems with which they have no real connection, and reminds one strongly of the continental Natureingang. In spite of arguments to the contrary[1] it still seems historically probable that the continental poetry could have become known in Wales, even in North Wales, by the mid-twelfth century through the medium of the Norman-French centres in the south. But the internal evidence of the poems is not very convincing. There are certain elements in the Gogynfeirdd poetry which do seem to be continental; notably the association of love-making with spring time, the occurrence of the nightingale particularly as the bird of spring and love,[2] and (much more doubtfully) the supposed appearance of the Jealous Husband and the Love Messenger. None the less the Gogynfeirdd poems as a whole cannot have been influenced extensively by continental poetry, or it would have left more of its characteristic traces upon them. The general probability of Irish imitation in Wales after the return of Gruffydd ab Cynan with his Irish bards from Ireland in 1075 has often been noted;[3] but the seasonal song seems to have declined in popularity in Ireland before the late eleventh century, and if there had been Irish influence we should not expect to find it limited to the seasonal beginnings, which as a genre are themselves quite un-Irish.[4] Some writers have tried to invent a hypothetical school of Welsh popular poetry contemporary with the Gogynfeirdd, songs

[1] See Chotzen, *Recherches*, pp. 14–21.

[2] The cuckoo is the characteristic spring bird in the native literature of these islands, and the nightingale in the Gogynfeirdd is no doubt a foreign trait, This is a matter on which much might be said.

[3] See C. O'Rahilly, *Ireland and Wales*, pp. 112 ff.

[4] But note that the later non-seasonal Irish poetry such as nos. XV and XVI, of a kind coming into prominence in the eleventh century, is often rather close in thought and style to the nature parts of the *gorhoffedd*.

"of spring and love, of flowery meadows and silvery mountain streams"[1] never recorded because the singers were not official court bards.[2] It is most unlikely that the court poets would have borrowed from such a school if it had existed, but actually there is no evidence that it did. There does in fact seem to have been a body of jongleurs and vagrant poets in mediaeval Wales, called *clerwyr* and *y gler*,[3] but it is not possible to show that they were known before the fourteenth century.[4] No doubt there were grades lower than the court bards before that time, the story-tellers who composed or adapted the Mabinogion and the englyn elegies and probably (as we have seen, pp. 138, 174–5) the early Welsh seasonal and gnomic poems in the same metre; but there is nothing to show that they wrote love poetry[5] and nature poetry of the kind described by Sieper and Chotzen. The school "of spring and love, of flowery meadows and silvery mountain streams" is a romantic fantasy of Sieper's evolved from the twelfth-century continental poetry and from the nature poetry of the present day.

The explanation offered here is intended merely as a suggestion. We saw that the Gogynfeirdd seasonal-beginnings were meagre and as it were conventional formulae attached to poems with which they were not really connected. This indicates perhaps that they are the last of a dying tradition; and it may be that the original nature song which was the

[1] "Von Lenz und Liebe, von blumiger Heide und silbernen Gebirgsbächen", E. Sieper, *Die Altenglische Elegie*, p. 58.

[2] Chotzen has attempted to reconstruct their poetry from modern Irish and Welsh folk poetry, but the gap of time is too great and modern folk literature too full of foreign and learned elements for this to be possible.

[3] Cf. Ifor Williams, *Detholion o Gywyddau Dafydd ab Gwilym*, pp. lxvi–lxvii.

[4] *Ibid.* p. lxvii.

[5] Chotzen (*Recherches*, p. 176) takes poem C for a love poem, which it certainly is not.

source of the englyn seasonal poetry, whether it was seasonal carols or what else, became a bardic fashion and passed as naturally into the early court poetry[1]—for court poetry there must have been before the time of the Gogynfeirdd—as into the different type of literature called the englyn poems; and hence it appears in the earliest Gogynfeirdd poems as a convention already somewhat worn. The association of elegy with natural scenery would help in the process and would explain why apparently unconnected nature-beginnings are found in some Gogynfeirdd elegies. It is to be noted that the May and Winter seasons are prominent, and even the Calends. This may then have been overlaid in the twelfth and thirteenth centuries with certain characteristics from the poetry of the French civilisation which the Welsh had learned to know and respect by that time, all the more easily because that poetry was considerably similar in its nature-beginnings to the Welsh convention already in existence.

Dafydd ab Gwilym, the chief of the succeeding "cywydd" school, is altogether too late to affect this discussion. The whole question of his sources is a much disputed one. Occasionally he writes as a Gogynfardd, and once or twice quotes or adapts the earlier englyn poems, but essentially he is himself alone, and his brilliant and whimsical nature poems have nothing in common with our early Welsh nature poetry.[2]

[1] But it is notably lacking in the Gododdin and the early bardic poems of Taliesin.

[2] The technique of *dyfalu*, describing something by a series of metaphorical comparisons, on which he lavished all his skill, has been derived from early riddling poetry; but it never appears in the englyn nature poems and in fact only one such riddle is known (see p. 86). It is presuming on the evidence to make Dafydd a representative of the earlier school on the strength of this (as Chotzen does, *Recherches*, p. 181), and it is most probable that it was Dafydd himself who had the originality to apply this technique first to the ordinary descriptive poem.

LIST OF CHIEF WORKS MENTIONED

C. APPEL, *Provenzalische Chrestomathie*, 4th ed. Leipzig, 1912.

K. BARTSCH, *Chrestomathie Provençale*, 4th ed. Elberfeld, 1880.

O. J. BERGIN, *Dictionary of the Irish Language*, fasciculus 2, ed. M. Joynt and E. Knott. Dublin, Royal Irish Academy, 1932.

—— and C. MARSTRANDER, *Miscellany Presented to Kuno Meyer*. Halle, 1912.

R. I. BEST and H. J. LAWLOR, *The Martyrology of Tallaght* (Henry Bradshaw Society, LXVIII). London, 1931.

H. M. and N. K. CHADWICK, *The Growth of Literature, vol.* I, *The Ancient Literatures of Europe*. Cambridge, 1931.

TH. CHOTZEN, *Recherches sur la Poésie de Dafydd ab Gwilym*. Amsterdam, 1927.

GLYN DAVIES, *The Welsh Bard and the Poetry of External Nature*, Transactions of the Honourable Cymmrodorion Society, 1912–13.

J. GWENOGVRYN EVANS, *The Black Book of Carmarthen* (Series of Old Welsh Texts, V). Pwllheli, 1907.

—— *The Text of the Book of Taliesin* (Series of Old Welsh Texts, IX). Llanbedrog, 1910.

—— *The Poetry in the Red Book of Hergest* (Series of Old Welsh Texts, XI). Llanbedrog, 1911.

SIR J. G. FRAZER, *The Golden Bough*, parts I–VII. Macmillan, 1911–15.

C. GREIN and P. WÜLCKER, *Bibliothek des Angelsächsischen Poesie*, 3 vols. Leipzig, 1881–98.

E. J. GWYNN, *The Rule of Tallaght* (Hermathena, XLIV, 2nd supplement). Dublin, 1927.

F. E. HOGAN, *Luibhleabhrán, Irish and Scottish Gaelic Names of Plants, Trees, etc.* Dublin, 1900.

—— *Onomasticon Goedelicum*. Dublin, 1910.

KENNETH JACKSON, *Early Welsh Gnomic Poems*. Cardiff, 1935.

A. JEANROY, *Les Origines de la Poésie Lyrique en France au Moyen Age*, 2nd ed. Paris, 1904.

J. MORRIS JONES and T. H. PARRY-WILLIAMS, *Llawysgrif Hendregadredd*. Oxford, 1933.

O. JONES, E. WILLIAMS and W. OWEN (PUGHE), *The Myvyrian Archaeology of Wales*, 2nd ed. Denbigh, 1870.

J. E. LLOYD, *The History of Wales from the Earliest Times to the Edwardian Conquest*, 2 vols. Longmans, Green and Co., 1903.

K. MEYER, *Bruchstücke der älteren Lyrik Irlands*, Abhandlungen der Preussischen Akademie der Wissenschaften, Berlin, 1919.
—— *Contributions to Irish Lexicography, A–DN* (Supplement to *Archiv für Celtische Lexicographie*). Halle, 1904–7.
—— *Four Old Irish Songs of Summer and Winter.* Nutt, 1903.
—— *Hibernica Minora, A Fragment of an Old Irish Treatise on the Psalter* (Anecdota Oxoniensia). Oxford, 1894.
—— *Selections from Ancient Irish Poetry.* London, Constable, 1911, 2nd ed., 1928.
—— and ALFRED NUTT, *The Voyage of Bran Son of Febal to the Land of the Living* (Grimm Library, no. 4). London, 1895.
G. MURPHY, "The Origin of Irish Nature Poetry", *Studies*, March, 1931, pp. 87 ff.
S. H. O'GRADY, *Silva Gadelica*, 2 vols. Williams and Norgate, 1892.
J. G. O'KEEFE, *The Madness of Suibhne Geilt* (Irish Texts Society, XII). London, 1913.
C. O'RAHILLY, *Ireland and Wales.* Longmans, Green and Co., 1924.
T. F. O'RAHILLY, *Dánta Grádha, An Anthology of Irish Love Poetry, 1350–1756*, with a preface by R. Flower, 2nd ed. Cork, 1926.
—— *Measgra Dánta, Miscellaneous Irish Poems*, 2 vols. (Irish Texts from MSS., vols. I–II). Cork, 1927.
C. PLUMMER, *Bethada Naem nErenn, The Lives of the Irish Saints*, 2 vols. Oxford, 1922.
—— *Vitae Sanctorum Hiberniae*, 2 vols. Oxford, 1910.
J. A. SCHMELLER, *Carmina Burana.* Stuttgart, 1847.
E. SIEPER, *Die Altenglische Elegie.* Strassburg, 1915.
WH. STOKES, *Félire Oengusso Céili Dé, The Martyrology of Oengus the Culdee* (Henry Bradshaw Society, XXIX). London, 1905.
—— and K. MEYER, *Archiv für Celtische Lexicographie*, 3 vols. Halle, 1900–7.
—— and J. STRACHAN, *Thesaurus Palaeohibernicus*, 2 vols. Cambridge, 1901–3.
R. THURNEYSEN, *Handbuch des Altirischen*, 2 vols. Heidelberg, 1909.
B. WILLIAMS, *Gnomic Poetry in Anglo-Saxon.* Columbia University Press, 1914.
I. WILLIAMS, *Canu Llywarch Hen.* Cardiff, 1935.
—— *Detholion o Gywyddau Dafydd ab Gwilym.* Bangor, 1921.
—— *The Poems of Llywarch Hen* (Proceedings of the British Academy, XVIII, Sir John Rhys Memorial Lecture for 1932). Humphrey Milford, 1933.

INDEX TO PART TWO

Agallamh na Senórach, the, 89, 116, 123, 124
Alba, the, 157 note 4
Alcuin, 158
"*A l'Entrade del Tens Clar*", 152
Alexandrians, the, 107–8
Almanacs, 164–70, 172
Amhrán metres, 153
Anchorite Rules, *see* Monastic Rules
Anchoritism, early Christian, 93–5
Andromache, the Lament of, 118
Anocht, see *Inocht*
Antiquarian Welsh proverb collections, 139–143
Antiquarianism, Irish, 124
Arfderydd, battle of, 111
Artemis, the Hymn to, 83
Arthur and the Eagle, the Dialogue of, 139
Asceticism, 98–100
Assembly of Tara, the, 95, 104

Barrinthus, the voyage of, 98
Beowulf, 116, 118, 131, 138
Bird song in calendars, 164–6
Boromha, the, 123
Bran, the voyage of, 83, 174–5
Brendan, the voyage of, 98
Brinkmann, 157–8

Calendar of Oengus, the, 85, 95, 99, 102, 122, 167
Canterbury Tales, the, 155
Caolite, 116, 124
Carmina Burana, the, 83 note 2, 150–1
Carolau haf, 162
Catonis Disticha, 140
Celtic Church, the early, 94–5
Céttamain, 160, 170, 178
Ciaran of Saighir, 94, 99, 101–2, 103
Coemgen, 97, 98, 107

Colman mac Duach, 97, 98
Columba, 90, 91, 92, 99, 104, 105, 122 note 1
Conaing, 91
Conflictus Veris et Hiemis, the, 158
Contests of Summer and Winter, 158–9, 162
Cromm Cruach, 161
Cúchulainn, 118
Cummene Fota, 121
Cyfarwyddiaid, the, 174
Cynddylan, 84, 117, 119, 120, 188

Dafydd ab Gwilym, 198
Dafydd Benfras, 193
Dál Araide, 111
Dancing in Mediaeval Ireland and Wales, 160–2
Dawnsio haf, 162
Deglán, 97
Deirdre, 89, 90, 91, 118, 126
"De Phyllide et Flora", 83 note 2
Devil's Tribute to Moling, The, 85
Dinnshenchas, the, 89, 124, 161
Duiblitir, 95

Einion ab Gwalchmai, 193
Eiry Mynydd poems, the late, 145–7
Englyn metre, the, 178, 181–6
Englynion y Clyweit, the, 139, 140, 141, 142, 183
Englynion y Misoedd, the, 163, 191
Ezra, auguries of, 172

Félire Oengusso Céli Dé, *see* Calendar of Oengus
Fenian poetry, 88, 89, 93 note 1, 123–6, 173, 175
Fer Diad, elegy on, 118
Fête de Mai, celebration of the, 156 note 1

INDEX

Fiana, the, 116, 124
Finn File, 173
Finn mac Cumhaill, 87, 88, 124, 162, 173, 174
Flower, Dr Robin, 95, 96, 102 note 2, 104, 106, 165
Folk songs, seasonal, 155–9
Food in Irish poetry, 125–6

Gam, 170
Gemeinschaftslied, the, 157, 158 note 1
Germanus, 94
Glen Bolcán, 122
Glossary of Cormac, 117, 160
Glyn Davies' theory of Welsh nature poetry, 176–81, 195
Gnome, definition of, 127
Gnomes, as classification, 135–6
   a semi-folk philosophy, 138
   composers of Welsh, 137
   in elegies, 131, 188
   in Heroic poetry, 131
   in Norse, 132
   not composed by clergy, 138–9
   the Cotton, 128, 163
   the Exeter, 128
   Welsh, date of, 141–5
Gobbán, 122
Gogynfeirdd, the, 193–8
Goliards, the, 150, 157
Gorhoffedd, the, 194, 195, 196
Gormflaith, 112–13, 120
Gossymdeith Llefoet Wynebclawr, 139, 147
Gruffydd ab Cynan, 160 note 6, 196
Guaire, 121
Guthrunarkvitha, 84
Gwalchmai, 193, 194
Gwalchmai and Tristan, dialogue of, 184, 185, 187

Hamthismál, the, 84
Hávamál, the, 132
Hector, elegy on, 119
Heno, 119–21

Hermits, clarity of vision of, 99
   huts of, 96–7
   ideals and characteristics of, 103, 105
   love of animals of, 100–3
   not authors of Welsh nature poetry, 178–81
   simplicity of, 107
   sincerity of, 104
Hesiod, 163–4, 166
Hitopadeça, the, 132 note 2
Homeric Hymns, the, 83
Homeric similes, 84
Honoratus, 94
Hymns to nature divinities, 82–3
Hywel ab Owain Gwynedd, 90, 194

Inocht, 119–21
Irish Dancer, The, 160
Irish influence on Welsh poetry, 177–81, 196

Juvencus manuscript, the Cambridge, 119

Kalan, 170
Kalan Gaeaf, 154, 160, 162
Kalan Mai, 160
Keen, the, 117–18
Kyntefin, 160, 170, 178

Llywarch ab Llywelyn, 193
Llywarch Hen, 114 note 3, 115, 116, 119, 147; 186
Llywelyn and Gwrnerth, dialogue of, 139, 185–6

Mab Claf, 147
Mac Coisse, 119
Mac da Cherda, *see* Moccu Cerda
Mac Samáin, 113 note 1, 123
Maedóc, 101, 103
Maelanfaid, 102
Maelodrán, 113 note 1, 122–3
Maelruain, 95, 102 note 2, 103, 104, 165

Maelsechlainn, 119
Manchín, 96, 98, 99, 100, 103, 105
Marbhán, 98, 99, 100, 107, 121
Marcolf, 147
Martyrologies, 167
May Day, 149, 150, 160, 161, 162, 190
Meigant, 139, 148
Menologium, the Anglo-Saxon, 167, 168, 169
Merlin, see Myrddin
Minnesingers, the, 150, 152, 157
Moccu Cerdda, 117, 121
Monastic Rules, 94, 95, 104, 105, 106
Myrddin, 111, 120, 121
Myvyrian Archaeology, the, 140, 148

Nature poetry, Irish, about places, 88–91
  Irish, imaginative, 81
  Irish, place names in, 124–5
  Irish, subjective, 80
  primitive, 79–80
Nature similes, 84–5
Natureingang, the, 150–8
Néde, prophecy of, 170–1
Nightingale in Gogynfeirdd poetry, the, 196

Old Woman of Beare, the, 115, 161

Pachomius and Palaemon, Rule of, 94, 104
Pan, the Homeric Hymn to, 83
Pangur Bán, 101
Pastoral, the, 152, 154
Patrick, 94
Paul the Deacon, 103
Pervigilium Veneris, the, 81, 82 note 1, 156 note 1
Piers Plowman, the Vision of, 155
Pindar, 88
Places, descriptions of, 88–91
Pleasant Things, 87, 195
Prophecies, 170–2
Proverbs in the Black Book of Chirk, 139

Proverbs in the Peniarth MS. 17, 139, 143
  in the White Book of Rhydderch, 139
  of Alfred, the, 147
  of Fithal, the, 133–4
  of Hending, the, 147
  of Hen Gyrys, the, 140, 142
Pseudo-Bede, the, 164–5

Quasi-gnomic poetry, 128, 176 and note 1

Rambaut de Vaqueiras, 152
Ratri, the Vedic Hymn to, 82
Retoric, 173
Riddles, 85–6
Ruin, The, 117
Runic Poem, the Anglo-Saxon, 86, 91

Saint Eloi, homilies attributed to, 156 note 1
Sam, 170
Samhain, 160, 161, 162
Sappho, 84
Scél lem dúib, 171
Seafarer, The, 113, 119, 168
Sea poetry, 91–2
Seasonal carols, 155–8
Seasonal poetry, authorship of, 172–5
Sickbed of Cúchulainn the, 133, 161
Sieper, Ernst, 79, 110, 196–7
Sieper's theory of the elegy, 118
Simple Life, the, 108
Solomon and Saturn, the dialogue of, 132, 134
Sons of Uisneach, the Fate of the, 89, 118
Suibhne Geilt, 97, 111 and note 4, 120, 121, 122
Swallow Song, the Rhodian, 156 note 1

Taliesin, 86, 87, 198 note 1
Theocritus, 88, 100, 108
Tiberianus, 81
Tigernach, 99

INDEX

Tuaim Inbhir, 97, 99, 122–3

Uc de la Bachelerie, 180
Urien, 117, 118, 119, 120

"Vagantes", the, 150
Vedic Hymns, the, 82
Verses of the Months, the, see *Englynion y Misoedd*

Vision literature, 154–5

Wanderer, The, 113, 117, 119
Weather, 170
Wife's Complaint, The, 114, 118, 119
Wild Man of the Woods, the, 111, 121–3
Winter's Day, 149